FURTHER PRAISE FOR

Travis Macy and *The Ultra Mindset*

"Immediately tangible and relevant, *The Ultra Mindset* uses engaging stories and clear advice to crystallize mindset principles for business and sports. I have enjoyed the results of applying these ideas to my own professional endeavors, and I'm confident you will too. Fun, motivational, actionable—that's *The Ultra Mindset.*

—JACK SWIFT, partner and managing director for Northern Lights Capital Group, elite mountain bike racer, and former West Point varsity runner and Army Ranger

"Racing through thick and thin around the world, Trav's positive outlook was second to none, and it played a big role in top finishes for our professional adventure racing team. The actionable concepts in this book are very relevant to life beyond racing."

—ROBYN BENINCASA, *New York Times* bestselling author of *How Winning Works* and World Champion adventure racer

"If you seek an improved mindset that will generate wellness and exceptional results in work, family, athletics, and beyond, then this is the book for you. Travis has achieved more in endurance sports over the last decade than many athletes hope to do in a lifetime, and I've always known that he had something important to teach us. Here it is."

—MARSHALL ULRICH, extreme adventure athlete, Seven Summits climber, and author of *Running on Empty*

"Running together years ago at CU–Boulder, I always wished I was able to look at my own training with Travis's balanced, glass-half-full perspective. In *The Ultra Mindset*, he shows us how we can push ourselves in all aspects of our lives while still having fun doing it."

—MATT MCCUE, author of *An Honorable Run*

"Insightful advice for all aspects of life from the man I like to call 'the Indiana Jones of adventure racing.' *The Ultra Mindset* is a way to share in Travis's adventures . . . and embark on your own."

—JOSIAH MIDDAUGH, professional triathlete and ten-time XTERRA USA National Champion

"*The Ultra Mindset* shows the way to maximize anyone's success in any area of life with poignant, colorful stories of pain and suffering in the athletic outdoors—and how they apply to the real world."

—DAVE MACKEY, UltraRunner of the Year, US National Champion for 100K Trail Running, 15:53 Master's course record at Western States 100

"As my endurance coach, Travis was THE reason I was able to recently complete my first ultramarathon. Travis is a regular guy who does amazing things simply by practicing what he preaches, and I guarantee this book will change your life."

—CHARLES MARTELLI, parent, sales professional, and amateur athlete

"Travis coached me to victory in the 2014 Leadman Series, so I know firsthand that his mindset principles are actionable and helpful not only in my athletic endeavors but also in my business and personal life."

—BOB AFRICA, kidrobot CEO and Leadman Champion

THE
ULTRA
MINDSET

THE
ULTRA
MINDSET

An Endurance Champion's 8 Core Principles
for Success in Business, Sports, and Life

Travis Macy *with* **John Hanc**

Da Capo
∞
LIFE
LONG

A MEMBER OF THE PERSEUS BOOKS GROUP

Book designed by Linda Mark
Set in 10.75 point ITC Giovanni Std by the Perseus Books Group

Library of Congress Cataloging-in-Publication Data
Macy, Travis.
  The ultra mindset : an endurance champion's 8 core principles for
success in business, sports, and life / by Travis Macy with John Hanc.
    pages cm
  Includes index.
  ISBN 978-0-7382-1814-4 (paperback)—ISBN 978-0-7382-1815-1
(e-book) 1. Success in business. 2. Success. 3. Successful people.
I. Hanc, John. II. Title.

  HF5386.M2344 2015
  650.1—dc23
                                                        2014042968

Published by Da Capo Press
A Member of the Perseus Books Group
www.dacapopress.com

Da Capo Press books are available at special discounts for bulk
purchases in the U.S. by corporations, institutions, and other
organizations. For more information, please contact the Special
Markets Department at the Perseus Books Group, 2300 Chestnut
Street, Suite 200, Philadelphia, PA, 19103, or call (800) 810-4145,
ext. 5000, or e-mail special.markets@perseusbooks.com.

10 9 8 7 6 5 4 3 2 1

For Wyatt and Lila.
I wish you happiness and resilience, and I love you.
Dad

Contents

Foreword

By Dean Karnazes

IN MY FIRST BOOK, *ULTRAMARATHON MAN*, I WROTE ABOUT MY colleagues and fellow travelers in what I called "the ultramarathon underground."

While the number of ultradistance runners has grown significantly since then—part of the overall, explosive growth in distance running in general—what I said about our somewhat exclusive fraternity in 2005 remains true a decade later. I wrote about the phenomenal level of dedication and commitment demonstrated by competitive ultra-marathoners, their ability to withstand pain, the fire in their hearts that keeps them going, and their high level of motivation. These things haven't changed.

I also talked about the fact that many ultra athletes run alone (think about it: How many other people want to join you for an eight-hour training jaunt?) and about how, in general, they tend to be a pretty reserved group of people.

Travis Macy, a member of the cadre of younger ultrarunners who are now dominating the sport, takes these ideas a step further (and, as ultrarunners, we're always ready to take further steps). Born and raised in the high-altitude Rockies, the son of the accomplished endurance athlete and adventure-racing and ultrarunning pioneer Mark "Mace" Macy, Travis is a sort of ultradistance-running (and biking) mountain man. He competes in races in the Rockies and the French Alps—that is, in places where it requires hiking poles to propel oneself up sheer cliffs, and where the air is so thin it would leave even a fit guy from sea level gasping for breath within minutes.

The mountains are Travis's domain. And up there, running alone high in the Rockies, he's had a lot of time to think. What he's brought down from the mountains for the rest of us—ultrarunners, distance runners, and nonrunners alike—is the realization that, as much as talent and physiology, it is a series of traits and attitudes that enables us to do the things we do in this sport.

Travis has organized these into what he calls the Ultra Mindset.

He believes (and just for the record, I agree) that the components of this mindset can be adopted by anyone and applied to almost anything in life. Not just running 100 miles, as Travis has done. Not just running the length of Zion National Park in Utah in a record-setting time, as Travis has done. Not just winning what some people call the Ultra of Ultras, the Leadman competition, which Travis has also done, and which involves competing in five ultradistance events in one short summer, capped off by back-to-back 100-mile mountain-bike and trail-run races (at altitude, naturally).

Prior to his current focus on running, Travis was also one of the best adventure racers in the world, racing year-round in multiday, nonstop competitions in places such as China, Argentina, France, New Zealand, and Brazil. If righting a flipped kayak in the middle of the night in an ice-lined Swedish river above the Arctic Circle, while thoroughly sleep-deprived, doesn't require extreme focus and mental toughness, I don't know what does.

This book teaches you how to right your own kayak: how to deal with adversity, surmount barriers, and overcome obstacles.

It also teaches you how to use the Ultra Mindset to approach the opportunities of life: things like why you should never quit—except when it's time to quit; how to take choice out of the picture when focusing on a goal; how to replace negative stories with positive ones (I could have used a couple of those when I was partway through the 135-mile Badwater Ultramarathon in Death Valley and it was 120°F); and about some other interesting and useful concepts for achieving your dreams and aspirations.

Travis talks in this book about the importance of knowing your strengths and weaknesses and asking for help when need be, as evidenced by his reaching out to John Hanc for writing support. Like me, Hanc has run a marathon in Antarctica (and wrote a book on it, *The Coolest Race on Earth*). He is an accomplished writer who has been writing about running and self-improvement topics for decades. Together John and Travis have created a highly readable and highly useful book that not only tells the tale of Travis's adventurous life— and how he forged the ideas that became the Ultra Mindset—but also shares relevant stories, principles, and activities to help you develop a similar mindset of your own. Their suggestions are as meaningful to corporate CEOs, young professionals, and stay-at-home parents as they are to runners and ultrarunners, triathletes, and other sports enthusiasts.

I gave the last chapter of *Ultramarathon Man* the forward-looking title "Run for the Future." I think that is exactly what this book can do for you: provide you with the tools, not to mention that spark of inspiration, to move ahead confidently into the future, *your* future. Whether that future includes running or mountain biking or adventure racing is largely beside the point. The point is that those same organizing principles that allow those of us in "the ultramarathon underground" to cross the finish lines of our long-distance ambitions can also help you achieve your dreams.

That is the true gift Travis shares with us.

Dean Karnazes
SAN FRANCISCO
OCTOBER 2014

The French Alps

JULY 2014

"I've got to do this."

"Are you crazy? You're feeling good and you've got third place locked up!"

"But they made a big deal about these rules before the race. I don't want to get disqualified."

"You won't be. We've been out here for seven hours . . . climbed two mountains, run across a glacier. We're almost done. Nobody is going to say a thing."

"But what if they do a gear check at the finish line and I get DQ'ed right there, with Wyatt watching? How do you explain that to a three-year-old? 'Daddy broke the rules, and he got caught, so you see it's okay to break the rules sometimes, just don't get caught?' That's great advice!"

"Dammit, you flew 5,000 miles to compete in this race. You've earned it."

"And what about my students? How do I tell them about this in September?"

"Your students know you . . . and they think what you do is pretty cool. But if you turn around now, they'll think you're a fool. What kind of lesson is that?"

"The lesson is that you have to do the right thing. And I have to do this."

If this argument had gone on much longer, it might have led to blows. That would have been interesting, as I would have had to punch myself in the mouth, right there on the steep, snowy slopes of the Col de Lessieres. Right there in the last 4 miles of this oxygen-starved, 40-mile, mountain ultramarathon known as the ITT—the Ice Trail Tarentaise.

I really did have this conversation within my head—albeit in the course of a few seconds—and it really was a tough decision. And with the proceedings now concluded, I reluctantly did something that few competitive racers of any distance in any sport ever do.

As the finish line was just coming into view in the distance, just down the hill in the valley below, glimmering with promise in the Alpine sunlight that had broken through the lower clouds, I turned around and began running back *up* the snowy mountain I had just sprinted down.

▲▲▲

THE LONGEST DISTANCE CONTESTED IN THE OLYMPIC GAMES IS THE 26.2-mile marathon. That's also about as far as most fitness and rec- reational runners go. It's plenty far and plenty challenging. But there's another whole classification beyond the marathon: ultrarunning. These distances start at 50 kilometers—around 31 miles—and continue up to 50 miles, up further to 100 kilometers, and then 100 miles, and . . . well, they even go further, into 24-hour and multiday runs. An "ultradistance event," put simply, is a race that's longer than 26.2 miles.

That's my territory. A realm not of just long distance, but *ultra* long distance.

While ultrarunning is currently my main sport, that's not the only way I traverse these super long distances. I have been a member of some of the world's top adventure-racing teams. These, as you may have seen on TV, are multiday race expeditions in remote or wild corners of the world, where teams of people run, paddle, rappel, and bike their way along a route they also have to navigate. I can pedal mountain bikes for a fair amount of time, and I've finished on the podium at 24 Hours of Moab, 24 Hours of Leadville, TransMexicana, and other endurance mountain-biking events. I love snowshoe racing in the winter, and I have also spent some time ski mountaineering, orienteering, rock climbing, and doing triathlons.

But there's another dimension to my running and biking and other endurance sports activity that is important to understand: Imagine a 30- or 50-mile stretch of road, and then imagine lifting up that road, draping it over a mountain range, and, to take your visualization one step further, wielding a sledgehammer and breaking up the smooth, even asphalt into a rocky trail. For good measure, throw in a snowstorm. Now you're in *my* world, one that I share with a cadre of like-minded endurance athletes who like to be sky high. This is the arena of mountain running and mountain endurance races; the world of icy trails and crevasses, of glaciers and snowcapped peaks, of loose rock and snowdrifts.

Saying that "the mountains are in my blood" might sound pretentious. But they are in my backyard: 7,500 to 10,000 feet is the altitude I typically train at when I'm home in Colorado. Whether it's training with a long run on Grays and Torreys Peaks, two of the so-called "14ers" (that's 14,000-foot peaks, of which Colorado has 54) just down the street from my house, or racing in a multiday, multisport race in Vail, I get excited for lengthy, challenging endeavors, and the air I breathe while doing so is even thinner than I am (and at 5 feet, 10 inches, 140 pounds, I'm pretty lean).

So I guess you could call me a professional, multisport, ultra-endurance mountain athlete. Or, as many have, you could just call me crazy. Crazy enough, I guess, to wake up at 2:15 on a Sunday morning to compete in the ITT on a day in mid-July in the French Alps, where it's still so cold that you need to wear a ski cap and gloves.

I am one of the elite athletes invited to compete today in this race, part of the Skyrunner Ultra Series, a popular circuit of mountain races in Europe. In the ultra world—a world, I should add, that has grown larger in the past few years, thanks to best-selling books by Dean Karnazes and Scott Jurek, and the "Born to Run" phenomenon—I am best known as the guy who won Leadman. This is a sort of six-week Grand Prix of Ultra Endurance that starts with a 26.2-mile trail marathon, followed by a 50-mile mountain-bike race, and then—in the course of seven days—a 100-mile mountain-bike ride, a 10K foot race the next day, and, in the grand finale the following weekend, the famed Leadville, Colorado, 100-mile ultramarathon. All of the events in the Leadman are contested at altitudes between 10,200 and 13,186 feet. The fastest overall combined time wins—which I managed to do in the summer of 2013 when I set a new Leadman record of 36 hours, 20 minutes.

In ultra circles, I'm also known for a record-breaking solo run: in April 2013, I ran 48 miles across Zion National Park in Utah in 7 hours, 27 minutes, 48 seconds. You might say, "Who even thought of the idea of speed records in Zion National Park?" I don't know, but I can tell you that this and similar FKT (Fastest Known Time) runs are very popular in the ultradistance community. Personally, I think it's pretty cool, even if my record was broken just a few months later.

Yet, while it's nice to have these kinds of achievements on my resume, the thing I'm most proud of is my consistency (or is it stubbornness?). In a decade-long career as a professional endurance athlete, I have completed 104 ultradistance events, roughly 10 a year, on foot, bike, snowshoe—and sometimes on horseback, kick-bike, canoe, kayak, raft, and other unique forms of adventure racing locomotion. I have won or finished in the winning team in about a quarter of these and was second or third overall in many more. I'm proud also to have finished each of the 11 multiday, nonstop "expedition" adventure races of four to seven days that I started with my coed teams of four people each. I'm not sharing these results because I want you to think I'm something special. In fact, it's more of the opposite: noteworthy ultra-endurance results by an otherwise fairly ordinary dad, husband, and working guy are part of the proof that the ideas in this book work. They have worked for me, and they can work for you.

While it's fun being a professional athlete in Colorado, it's not quite a living, unless maybe your name is Peyton Manning. I call it a second income. Most of my income comes from work in a few different teaching roles. I taught in traditional and online high-school English and P.E. classrooms for seven years before transitioning to running and executing a private college-admissions counseling business with my wife, coaching other adult endurance athletes, and training and motivating audiences through speaking and workshops. These roles are diverse, but they are all centered in teaching, which is what I'd been doing for most of my professional life, in one form or another. I love motivating and educating people, whether it's the adolescents I teach or the runners I coach or the corporate audiences I speak to. And I hope that now I can motivate *you*—and maybe teach you a thing or two that can help you in your endeavors, whatever they may be.

That's really the purpose of this book: to help you to achieve your goals—whether they are in racing or in life—by sharing with you a few of the principles that have held me in good stead as I've logged my ultra miles through mountains, forests, deserts, and jungles. Are you looking to complete your first marathon or century bike ride? Are you trying to qualify for Boston? Are you training for your first triathlon, or ultra, or charity 5K walk? Maybe you're trying to summon the courage to launch a new business, or enter a new career? Perhaps you just want to become a better parent, spouse, friend . . . person.

This book is about the Leadville Race Series and mountain biking in China and running across Utah and kayaking in Sweden and a whole lot more, because my experiences in these venues show that people really can accomplish whatever they commit to. I hope you'll find my racing stories interesting, and maybe even entertaining. But primarily, they are vehicles to deliver tangible, actionable principles that are relevant to you and your endeavors. Principles that have steeled me, supported me, and guided me through some very long and arduous miles, in very faraway places and difficult circumstances.

Principles that I call the Ultra Mindset.

Whatever the distance, whatever the level, whatever the scope of the achievement you want to reach, the Ultra Mindset can help you. I've seen how it can work, even if you never run a step.

And whether you're a runner or not, whether you're someone who understands or cares about split times and PR's and lactate threshold training and all the things we endurance athletes care about, or someone who wouldn't know a timing chip from a chocolate chip cookie, you can appreciate this: one thing I'm known for is finishing. Maybe not always in first place, but I always finish; I always go the distance in the races I enter (unless, as did happen, I'm in the hospital, or one of my teammates is. Hey, it happens!).

It's not because I'm so tough or determined, although sometimes you do have to dig deep in an ultra. No, the reason I finish is commitment: before every race, during my training, I have committed to finishing. I have removed the option of not reaching the finish line. If you make a similar, wholehearted commitment—in your racing, your career, your life—you will reach your goals, too.

This isn't just a rah-rah speech about how you can overcome any obstacle. You and I know full well that there are some obstacles we can't conquer, no matter how hard we try. But I've never met an obstacle yet—be it crevasse or icy mountain slope; or, for that matter, difficult exam or pain-in-the-ass boss—that can't be sized up, broken into manageable chunks, taken on, and eventually overcome.

Similarly, this isn't just another bromide about giving it your all and never quitting. I told you a moment ago that I have finished 104 ultradistance races, and only DNF-ed (that's race parlance for "Did Not Finish") in two, both times due to injury. But I *have* quit a few non-racing endeavors over the years, and in these cases letting go of an outdated and less-than-ideal goal actually took a lot more courage than continuing to plod ahead on a course that did not align with my greater purposes in life. As I've learned in adventure racing, when we have to plot our courses through vast stretches of wilderness, there is a time to dig deep and forge ahead. And then there are times to go a different route. Overcoming fear is an integral—and often challenging—element of rewriting internal stories and changing your course for the better: I hope you learn that on the pages that follow.

What I call the Ultra Mindset is a little different from the typical and often well-meaning advice you might hear from coaches or self-help gurus. It's realistic advice. While it is informed by some interesting psychological research into human motivation, resilience, and positivity, I am not a psychologist. However, I do know something about how to endure, how to suffer, and how to complete the task at hand.

In each section of the book, my coauthor John Hanc and I relate some of the experiences I've had as a racer, charting the course of my life as a mountain ultra-endurance athlete along the way, to illustrate to you each one of the principles. In the second half of each chapter,

I discuss in more depth how you can use that same principle—or Mindset—to help yourself. Because some of these Mindsets involve changes in outlook or attitude, I'll offer some self-assessments and exercises to help you make the often subtle but potentially significant shift needed. I've provided workouts that are crucibles for this kind of ultra thinking (and no, the workouts are not all ultradistance; they're geared for people of all ability levels). Finally, in each chapter you'll also hear from an elite endurance athlete whom I admire. These contributors will tell you, in their own words, how they apply the various aspects of the Ultra Mindset to their own sports and lives.

The eight principles of the Ultra Mindset have been used not only by me and other athletes I know but also by many of the people I've coached. But remember: You don't have to be training for an ultra-endurance race to harness the power of the Ultra Mindset! You can use these concepts to successfully get through the mental and physical barriers in your first marathon, 10K run, century bike ride, or charity walk.

But, much as I get excited to hear about anyone finishing his or her first anything in the world of endurance activities, it is my belief that you can apply these same concepts to other aspects of your life, which to me is the real value of this book. Properly applied, the principles of the Ultra Mindset can help you in your job, in your relationships, in whatever it is you want to do with your life.

Where is that life going? Maybe you're in a good place, simply looking to make it even better. But you may also be struggling with something—motivation, relationships, fitness, career, addiction, whatever—right now. Or maybe the struggle is with something not done, the road not taken. Perhaps you are intimidated by the things you would like to do or need to do—overcome by reasons not to do them, afraid of commitment, dragged down by negative stories, unsure about what you want to do or who you want to be, or standing on the brink of something monumental and barely conceivable. (I've been all of those other places before, both in racing and in life, and I've found my way through.) As Dr. Seuss says in my son Wyatt's favorite book, *Oh the Places You'll Go*, it's inevitable that at times in life, you'll be "left in a lurch."

The book you hold in your hands is written to get you going, and to remind you that, "Kid, you'll move mountains." It will show you how to think and act in order to do just that—to get out of that lurch and into the high ground.

Wherever you are now in relation to where you want to be, this book is for you, dear reader, and your journey to a winning outlook and peak performance in relationships, work, fitness, and anywhere else you seek growth.

And this book—and the Ultra Mindset—might come in especially handy when those beliefs, those core principles, that commitment, is tested in unexpected, unsettling ways. As they were for me in the French Alps.

▲▲▲

VAL D'ISÈRE: THE ITT

From the start of the ITT, the top guys went out hard, climbing a gradual uphill on a wet, paved road through the ski resort of Val d'Isère, a town that is snowbound five months a year, and shows it: we breezed by the tony ski and apparel outfitters—the North Face, Oakley, and Columbia outlets—and into the looming darkness surrounding the resort town. I checked my Garmin GPS watch: we kept a 5:30-per-mile pace as we rolled through the town flats. A little fast for this early in the race—a lot of testosterone out here today, I thought.

Soon we were on a trail with a herd of horses grazing nearby. As they sensed us, some of them instinctively galloped along with us for a short while, their hooves splashing water against our legs as we crossed a stream in unison, a convergent herd of runners and horses. They made it look easy. We kept going.

At this point, I was in the lead pack of about eight to ten guys. The pace was fast, but I was feeling fairly comfortable. We began to gain altitude, climbing a steep and now muddy single track from Val d'Isère and then up above the village of Tignes. I could see our rental apartment building below, and although I didn't know it at the time, my wife, Amy, was already up and scanning the horizon for a distant line of runners. Then came a long descent on a rocky trail, made muddier by the rain. I realized then that, despite my careful packing and check-listing, I had made a mistake with my gear: my headlamp wasn't powerful enough for this race. Although the trail was well marked with orange flags, I could barely see a few feet in front of me. Soon, I lost contact with the lead pack, most of whom had gone helter-skelter down that trail.

This was the first opportunity for freaking out, but experience in long races told me to remain calm. "Keep the faith," as my dad used to say, and you will usually end up all right, as long as you stay positive and don't give up on yourself. I knew from the reconnaissance runs I'd done of the racecourse that we were about to hit a long uphill. I'm pretty confident in my climbing abilities, so I reassured myself that falling behind a bit at this early stage of the race was okay. While the peak elevation we would achieve on the upcoming climb—11,984 feet—is very high for the Alps, I'm lucky to run well above that elevation in Colorado on a regular basis. As for some of those guys who'd thundered down the trail ahead of me, I had a feeling I'd be seeing them again soon.

I was right. We began the ascent of the mountain known as the Grand Motte, the highest climb of the race. We were already at 6,890 feet, and over the next 3 miles or so we gained an additional 5,094 feet. The route we followed up the side of the mountain was a groomed ski slope. I almost smiled when, at about 7,500 feet, we hit the snow. This played to my strengths. All winter this is what I train on, racing up and down snow-covered mountains, on and off ski slopes in iconic Rocky

Mountain locations like Vail, Beaver Creek, Aspen, and Winter Park. As soon as I felt the familiar crunch of snow under my feet, I stopped to slide my Kahtoola NanoSpikes, traction devices that function like mini-crampons, to the outsoles of my shoes. They felt good digging into the snow, and with these, combined with my poles, which I had out now, I fell into an almost machine-like, propulsive rhythm, legs and arms moving. Repeating them like a silent mantra, I went through the motions, over and over, as we climbed:

> *Reach up and forward with the poles—pull down with both arms—push down with the left foot—drive the right knee up and forward—dig into the snow with the right foot.*

> *Reach up and forward with the poles—pull down with both arms—push down with the right foot—drive the left knee up and forward—dig into the snow with the left foot.*

On steep inclines like this, running becomes more like power hiking—or an outdoor Stairmaster.

I soon passed a couple of the guys who had run away from me on that dark descent. Now I could make out the runners in the lead. I recognized the tall, lean figure in first: François D'Haene, a 29-year-old gazelle—actually a physical therapist with a sideline in wine making—from Beaujolais, France. François has won the ITT and the super-competitive Ultra Trail du Mont Blanc, another legendary, 103-mile mountain run in the Alps. I knew I probably wasn't going to be able to catch him here. Maybe if these were the familiar trails around Vail, I'd have an outside chance, but this was his home turf.

The second-place guy looked to be struggling. In the gathering light behind the clouds and mist that seem a permanent part of the landscape in the high Alps, I saw a silhouette of diminishing energy. Each step he took looked shorter and slower than the last, and instead of pushing powerfully on the poles, he appeared to be leaning on

This shot from one of my training runs on the Ice Trail course shows just how harsh the July conditions can be in the French Alps. After taking this photo, I turned around to get back to town before getting stuck in a blizzard in unfamiliar terrain. CREDIT: TRAVIS MACY

them to keep from falling down. I felt bad for him—all of us in this sport know what it's like to suffer—but in terms of the race, this was good for me. One more competitor I could pass.

Near the top there was an almost miraculous moment: the fog lifted, the low-hanging clouds seemed to part, and suddenly I was running in the go n sunlight reflecting off the white peak of the Grand Motte, with a brilliant blue sky in the background. I was working hard at this point. I had many miles to go, and I knew I would experience the inevitable lows known to every ultrarunner, but at this moment I felt grateful to be here and privileged to be able to do this. Down in Tignes and Val d'Isère, back across the ocean and half a continent away in Colorado, many people I knew were asleep in bed, and I was up here touching the edge of heaven.

My spiritual reverie was short-lived. As the once-popular bumper sticker used to remind us, "S—t Happens," and in ultramarathons, it happens a lot. Let's use, as an example, a last-minute course change. Changing the course of, say, the New York City Marathon on the morning of the race would practically take a mayoral edict. But in a mountain race like the ITT, changes in the unpredictable Alpine weather can affect everything, and in a snap. The original plan of this race was to go to the very top of the Grand Motte. But because of unstable snow conditions that could have resulted in an avalanche near the summit, the race organizers had decided that morning to adjust the course. We had only been informed at the start. Just below the peak, but still on top of the world, we were to turn around and head back down the way we came.

Imagine running full speed down a double-diamond-level ski course. You're not really running, you're scrambling, then sliding, like a baseball player stealing second, except here the baseball diamond is tilted, and you're sliding all the way to home plate. Sounds like fun, but you have to be careful when you get to lower altitudes, and the snow gives way to rocks. And because you can run faster than you can slide, you're still trying to run. I was up and down on the descent: upright as I did a shuffle run, trying to fend off gravity that wanted to suck me down the slope, and then, at points when it got too steep, sliding. I fell many times—par for the course, almost everyone did—scratching up my arms, hands, and legs, but avoiding serious injury.

I was about halfway through the race, and I was cruising along now, feeling good.

We stayed mostly off the road and instead ran along muddy, and—as we got higher—snowy trails. The covering varied. I'm a connoisseur of snow: there's soft and fluffy snow; there's hard and frozen snow; and then there's the stuff we found along a few narrow ridgelines here—hard on top, soft on bottom. The kind of snow where you can take ten steps, and then on the eleventh, you step through

There was a heck of a lot of snow along the rocky and mountainous Ice Trail course in France. At this point near the famed Col de l'Iseran, at a glacial ski slope that remained open in mid-July, the rocks met the snow. We had to be ready to run on a variety of types of terrain, and there were many points where I sank to my knees in the snow.
CREDIT: ALEXANDRE GARIN

the thick crust into soft, wet stuff underneath. Again, I felt right in my element, as opposed to an Australian runner I talked with afterward, who, coming from a land of little or no snow, was befuddled by this strange new substrate.

People often ask me what I'm thinking about when I run. One answer: food. Not just the post-race meal that all of us fantasize about—for me it's a burger and French fries—but the calories that are going to sustain me for the race. My goal in an ultra is to take in 250 to 300 calories per hour. So at the ITT, I was sucking down the Vitargo carb drink that I use, and at each of the five aid stations, I stopped briefly to wolf down a few pieces of the dark and exquisite French chocolate they were giving out and a few bites of the local salami and cheese (no, I don't eat like this all the time, but in an ultra it's all about fuel, not to mention taste cravings). At each station, volunteers were standing around, clad in heavy coats and ski hats—the temperature was just below freezing—ready to applaud every arriving racer. Some of the volunteers had cowbells, which they rang with great enthusiasm.

"*Allez, allez,*" they cried. "Go, go." I felt like I was in the Tour de France. The volunteers' enthusiasm, their unfamiliar language, and the allure of the vast, foreign mountains energized me.

I was *allez*-ing, all right. Going strong, feeling great. Road or track racers usually have a strategy before a race. They know where they're going to push; where they're going to hold back; where they're going to make their finish kick. In an ultra, because everything is played out for such an extended period of time, you have to pay attention more to how you're feeling. The strategy becomes simple: when you feel bad, try to hold on; when you feel good, it's time to push. It was time for me to push.

With just one more big climb to go in the Ice Trail, I was focused and ready to go!
CREDIT: ALEXANDRE GARIN

Early in the race, I'd noticed a stern-faced, square-jawed runner with close-cropped hair and sunglasses go whizzing past me on that initial downhill. He looked like the Terminator, like a young Arnold with ski poles. I began rolling an idea around in my mind, as I spotted him now, struggling, teeth gritted, sunglasses spattered with snow, ahead of me.

"Terminate the Terminator," I said to myself. "Terminate the Terminator."

Now, I had nothing against this guy—in fact, we chatted later, after the race, and he was warm and pleasant, very un-Terminator-like. But in a competition, you need to find ways to motivate yourself mentally, to help your body endure the pain that comes with pushing (even when you feel good). He provided just that.

Up and down the mountains we went, like elevators in a high rise, as the morning wore on. Ten miles, 20 miles, 30 miles. At about 34 miles—with a little over 6 to go—it was time to go back up yet again. This time we would ascend the Col de l'Iseran. At 9,800 feet, it's the highest paved mountain pass in the Alps, which is one reason it's a mountain that's been used numerous times by the organizers of the Tour de France (most recently in 2007).

Meanwhile, I had heard at one of the aid stations that the second-place guy behind D'Haene had dropped out. I was whittling my way down into the top five. Things were setting up nicely. I was still feeling strong, and we were coming to a climb. I sensed that I might be able to push, and as some of the other top guys seemed to be flagging, I could gain ground. I had one big hill, up and down, to go. Over the course of 7 kilometers, or 4.35 miles, I would ascend 2,250 feet to Aguille Pers, another mountaintop glacier at 11,109 feet, and then drop the same amount down the other side. I knew I could catch some guys here.

Now it was time for my secret weapon: music.

I must say that I don't typically bring music with me. In some road races, headsets are not allowed, and I'm a guy who always plays by the rules. But in an off-road race like the ITT, no one cares if you whip out your iPod and blast some tunes. I had my shuffle songs ready, carefully chosen to create the right mood at this point in the race: they were all upbeat songs designed to help distract me from the pain and help keep my foot turnover brisk. When I need an extra shot in the last part of a race, like a double espresso from the Italian moka pot I bought weeks prior in Spain, I turn to this. It helps me really start hammering.

The songs included an eclectic range of tunes and artists: Eminem, Neil Young, Katy Perry, Michael Jackson. I listened to "Gangnam Style" and that goofily upbeat song "Happy" by Pharrell Williams. I even rolled out that old chestnut of motivational workout songs, "Eye of the Tiger," from the movie *Rocky III*. So I was humming as I ran along, "rising up the challenge of our rivals," and passing more of those rivals as I rode this wave of music down the Col de l'Iseran. A race official along the trail raised three fingers when I passed: third place. Yes. *Oui!*

I was now on the final downhill: 3,855 feet to go over 5.6 miles. It had warmed up a bit, and I'd taken my jacket off and stuffed it into my backpack, next to the small crampons—my Kahtoola NanoSpikes—that I'd removed as soon as we got off the snow.

As I bolted downhill, I felt the backpack shifting. I looked over my shoulder and saw the zipper flapping: I hadn't fully zipped it back up. I stopped, unslung the bag, and saw an empty space where the Kahtoolas had been. "Damn," I thought. "They must have just fallen out. They have to be right here somewhere." But they weren't right there. I jogged back a few steps. Still no spikes. Part of me instinctively wanted to forget about them and just keep going down the hill to finish the race. There were now only about 4 miles left. In an ultra, that's like a final lap on the track.

This was where I had my internal debate about lost mandatory gear and the rules, and, in a larger sense, about right and wrong. The day before, in a pre-race meeting for all competitors, the organizers had made a big deal about mandatory gear. They'd paid a great deal of attention—as far as I could tell, with my limited French—to the crampons. They'd held one up for everyone to see. They'd even specified the brand—Yaktrax—and at the end of the meeting, I'd had to go show mine, a different brand, to the race director. He approved, but the message was clear: these guys were serious about the gear.

Or were they? I realized no one had checked my bag at the start. And while I certainly understood the need for the equipment and for taking precautions in these potentially dangerous conditions, we were now out of the higher altitudes and nearing the finish line. Would they really care now? Or, I thought darkly, would there be an equipment check at the finish line?

Above all, I thought, am I doing the wrong thing if I don't go back and look for them? Certainly, I hadn't lost the crampons on purpose, but I had lost them. Shouldn't I make an effort to retrieve them?

I decided that the answer to that question was yes. In part, because I was still sure that they couldn't be far back up the trail.

I was wrong. Once I turned around, and began laboring up the trail, craning my neck left and right looking for foot-length pieces of rubber with little grommets sticking out of them, in the vastness of a mountain slope, I began to realize how wrong. A minute went by. Two minutes. Meanwhile, one . . . then two of the guys I'd passed now passed me. "What is wrong?" one of them asked in French-accented English. "My traction device," I said. "Have you seen them?" He looked at me oddly and shook his head.

More running back up the trail. More craning of my neck. Still no Kahtoolas.

Then the Terminator came running along. He looked shocked to see me. I pointed to my foot, "Kahtoolas . . . er, Yaktrax," I said. "Have you seen these?" He just shook his head and gestured for me to come with him and continue running.

I shook my head no—ruefully—and continued back up the trail. Finally, I found them, sticking out of the snow. They had obviously gone flying out of my pack when I neglected to zip it all the way closed. It had taken me almost nine minutes to retrieve these stupid things. Now I was flying back down the hill, my internal debate resumed—and this time, reverberating with incriminations.

"Idiot," one voice said. "You blew this race."

Though I had gone from exhilaration to despair in a matter of minutes, another voice rose in my mind: "Come on, Trav, we never give up. Come on, Trav, we never give up! *Come on Trav, we never give up!*" The voice was quiet at first, but I soon found myself chanting aloud. Running down a steep, grassy ski hill just above town, I was currently alone, but I knew that if I didn't get things going—and immediately—I'd soon get passed by even more competitors.

When I finally crossed the finish line back in Val d'Isère, I was in sixth place, with a time of 8 hours, 13 minutes—about 35 minutes behind D'Haene, the winner. Three guys had passed me while I'd been retrieving the lost gear. As a result, I'd dropped from third to sixth in the last 4 miles of the race, and that was a huge disappointment.

After I crossed the line, I stopped and leaned on my poles, staring down at the ground as I pondered what had transpired. I saw two running shoes pointing at me and looked up. It was the Terminator. "What happened?" he asked in thickly accented English, sounding genuinely concerned. I explained as best as I could about the crampons, the rules, my fear of breaking them. He just made a face, shaking his head dismissively.

"You should have come with me," he said. "You were running well!"

I began to think he was right, as I realized what *hadn't* happened at the finish line. There was no gear check, no stern-faced officials with clipboards going through bags to ensure compliance. The crowd, the

Anyone who crosses the finish line in a race like the Ice Trail is ready to be done for the day. I was also grappling with a range of mixed emotions about the race I had just run, especially the abrupt shift from putting the hammer down on my competitors to running back uphill in search of lost mandatory gear just a few miles before the finish. CREDIT: ALEXANDRE GARIN

officials, the announcers were all enjoying this, applauding the runners as they crossed the line, blowing on air horns, ringing their cowbells, swaying in the rhythm of rap music blasting over huge speakers amid the party-hearty atmosphere of the finish area. Beers were being sipped, bottles of wine uncorked. And there I was in the midst of the festivities, an unsettled figure who had made a questionable choice. I felt like a philosopher in an existential crisis, while everyone else around me was simply enjoying life. Physically, the race had gone very well for me, and I'd had that *"this almost feels easy"* racing sensation as I'd moved up through the field during my late-race push to third place. Mentally, I had raced smart, taking care of myself and pushing hard at the right times, calculating effort and exertion with expert precision . . . but the turnaround for the lost mandatory gear had cost me bigtime.

Was this an ethical dilemma I should have even been grappling with in the midst of an intense race? Was this an example of me taking my commitment to always doing the right thing to an absurd extreme? Just what was the "right thing" anyway?

I heard my name: it was Amy and the kids. No time for pouting now—there's usually not—and little time for recovery. After a few hugs, and a shower and a meal, it would be back to dad duty.

That night at 2:00 a.m., almost 24 hours after I woke up on race day, I should have been sleeping deeply due to exhaustion, but my decision and race finish were replaying endlessly in my mind and the inner voices kept sleep at bay:

> *You should have thought it through . . . a real competitor doesn't worry about fine points of ethics coming down the homestretch of a major international race. You had a podium spot in a big mountain running race in Europe—something rarely achieved by Americans—and you blew it.*

Tossing and turning, upset with myself, I began to hear another voice as my internal debate was again joined. Unlike the strident voices that echoed through my head in midrace, this one started as a tentative whisper, but steadily grew in confidence and volume:

> *Enough second-guessing, enough rehashing, enough beating yourself up. Accept the choice you made today. Learn from it, stop feeling sorry for yourself, stay positive, recommit to doing your best with training, racing, parenting, work, writing that book, and the other things that matter to you.*

The Ultra Mindset had spoken. I shut my eyes, rolled over, and slept peacefully.

▲▲▲

SEVEN WEEKS LATER, RECOVERED, REENERGIZED, AND REFOCUSED, I competed in the Ultra Race of Champions: the Ultrarunning World Championship, a 100-kilometer mountain race in Colorado with some 10,000 feet of climbing at elevations of between 9,800 and 12,400 feet. Late in the race, I found myself once again in third place in a very competitive, national-class field. I thought about *what* I was doing in order to stay on top of nutrition, and I thought about *why* I was doing it to keep my motivation high. I told myself positive stories, intentionally reappraising the situation when I began to struggle and needed to bounce back. I thought about the commitment to finishing that I had made to myself, and how that commitment categorically removed quitting as an option. I held tough physically and mentally, exorcising the demons from Val d'Isère, and this time, there were no internal debates, no second guesses, no frantic searches for self, or, for that matter, traction devices.

I finished a strong third in the championship race.

The power of the Ultra Mindset is hard to contain once you understand and know how to harness it. So let's get started!

It's All Good
Mental Training

"KEEP HAMMERING, TRAVIS! WE DON'T STOP UNTIL WE get to the top of the hill!"

Rattling along a washboard road among the lodge-pole pine trees of Evergreen, Colorado—a mountain town 40 miles west of Denver—my father turned on the saddle of his mountain bike and looked over at me. His eyes covered by his Oakleys, his wispy brown hair streaking out from under his short-billed white racing cap, he smiled and nodded his head in the direction we were headed. He was saying, "I believe in you. You can do it."

I remember how I picked up the pace, navigating my little kid's mountain bike right behind him, where all I could see from my perspective underneath my tyke-sized helmet were the knobs on his tires and the veins of his powerful calf muscles.

It was July 1988, and I was five years old. It's one of my earliest memories—and in retrospect, I can see it's where the Ultra Mindset was forged. He and I biked like this regularly. It was our version of playing catch in the backyard. My dad liked all sports. He had played lacrosse in college, but by this point, distance running and triathlon were his favorites. In 1986, he'd even finished the Ironman triathlon in Hawaii—a 2.4-mile swim, 112-mile bike ride, and 26.2-mile run that many athletes still consider the most impressive multisport endurance achievement in the world.

A lawyer, Dad was typical of a lot of men who came of age in the 1970s. Inspired by the victory of Frank Shorter—himself a Yale graduate and a lawyer—in the 1972 Olympic Marathon, a whole generation of professional, white males like Dad had laced up their sneakers and primitive running shoes and taken to the roads, sparking what is often called the first "running boom."

Endurance sports became their choice for fun, fitness, and pushing limits, and it just so happened that my dad had a talent for it. Mark Macy—known to everyone else as "Mace"—biked and swam, too, and ten years before anyone had heard of Lance Armstrong, he was already a fan of the Tour de France.

Earlier in the ride, during the part that was supposedly fun, Dad rode just behind me as I struggled up a steep hill, encouraging me. "You can do it, Bud," he said, using his nickname for me.

And I did it.

While it might have looked like we were in the middle of nowhere, we were actually still biking through our neighborhood, which consisted of houses speckled in the woods along a network of dirt roads that wound up and around the foothills. There was not a block grid or paved road in sight. TV came in for all of the houses through a lone, 4-foot antenna atop the hill we were climbing. Mt. Evans, one of Colorado's massive 14,000-foot peaks, loomed over our roof. Limited phone lines meant that multiple houses shared a "party line." After all, Evergreen wasn't even an official town; it was an unincorporated community in Jefferson County. We didn't have a town hall, a movie theater, or any fast-food restaurants—we didn't even have a mayor!

I figured everyone lived in a place like this; that kids all over the world were also out "hammering the hills" with a tall, rangy, athletic dad; and that everyone had a choice of four channels on one TV and one phone line to share with four families.

We pushed up those hills, riding side by side, to help me go hard and push my limits. But Dad wasn't some kind of two-wheeled tyrant. He knew not to push a five-year-old too hard, and he also realized that we had to have fun. Dad's real goal here was not to make me a tough biker, but to help me develop the resilience that would carry me through other areas of life.

Having climbed the first pitch of our neighborhood hill, Dad and I came to the flat segment that marked the mid-stage sprint. On our limited menu of television, we had been able to watch the Tour de France, and I had become entranced with it. Dad was knowledgeable and had explained the intricacies of the fabled race. I knew the names of the top riders, including one of my early heroes, American Greg LeMond, who had won the 1986 Tour (and would return to win in 1989 and 1990 as well). So as my little legs pedaled vigorously, Dad imitated the BBC English voice of the incomparable Tour announcer Phil Liggett calling one of the stages.

"It's Fignon, LeMond and Hinault, side by side!" Dad would call, referring to LeMond's rivals Laurent Fignon and Bernard Hinault, other great Tour riders of that era. "Hinault takes the lead, but here comes LeMond. He's pulling away. It's . . . *LeMond*! He wins the stage at the line. What a finish!"

I thrust my hands skyward, blowing kisses to imaginary crowds. Dad would chuckle, and on we would pedal through the brilliant Colorado morning.

The road kicked up and got even rockier as we left our neighborhood and headed into the woods that surrounded Evergreen. I grunted. Well, probably squeaked—I was five. A burro inside the barbed-wire corral on the hillside brayed. We were now climbing what appeared, from my height-challenged vantage point, to be a very large hill, if not a mountain. My rear tire spun in the loose stuff, but I gained traction and continued. These were mountain bikes with rigid forks (front suspension was not yet widely available), so every rock I rolled over made my young bones shake. I was pushing, pushing. It hurt and I wanted to stop and go back and pretend to be Greg LeMond waving to the crowds some more. Just as I was about to put a foot down and stop in mid-climb, Dad tucked in next to me, his calm voice articulating what would become a recurring theme in my endurance education.

"You can do it, Bud," he said. "Don't stop on the climb. Commit to it. Hammer the hills. It's all good mental training, Bud."

Looking back on those days now, I'm not sure if I knew what the word "commit" meant at that age; and I'm sure I had no concept of "mental training." But I knew this much, and it's why the memory stays with me: I made it to the top of a hill that had looked impossible.

Dad believed in me, and that made me believe in myself.

Blast from the Past: Dad's First Leadville 100

I have another, related memory from 1988. Oddly enough, it was only a few weeks after my training ride with Dad. I think the reason I remember it, though, is because in a sense it vindicated the lesson I had learned on the hills of Evergreen on my little mountain bike; it sealed the deal, so to speak, and made me realize that not only could my dad cajole me up a hill and do a good imitation of Phil Liggett, but that he could back it up.

It was my second lesson in mental training. And it took place in America's highest incorporated city, Leadville, Colorado, which is lo-

Believe in Yourself

I had fun running and biking with Dad from the start. Mom took this shot after we finished the Talkeetna Moose Dropping Festival 5K in Alaska in 1994. CREDIT: M ACY FAMILY

cated at 10,200 feet in the Rockies. (Yes, Leadville has a mayor, and in the old days he was probably the kind of guy who wore a Stetson and carried a gun.)

Dad, who had never run more than a marathon, signed up for, committed to, and embarked upon the Leadville Trail 100 Run.

I was there, and I watched it unfold.

Looking back on our first Leadville 100—later it became somewhat of a family reunion for us—I realize it's incredible that we were even going to the race in the first place, and that we left with a somewhat intact father accompanying us.

It all started out like a holiday. As we drove down Little Cub Road in Dad's truck on the way to Leadville—which is located in the heart of the Rockies, at the base of Colorado's highest peak, Mt. Elbert—Mom turned around to give some special presents to my sister, Katelyn, and

I was an active little kid, and I always enjoyed going to Dad's races. CREDIT: MACY FAMILY

I, suitable for the occasion. We each received race clothes: KK, as we called her, got a shirt and shorts, and I got leopard tights and a black, sleeveless shirt, on the front of which was an image of a mountain lion (they frequented our neighborhood, and I wanted to pet them, which I was told would be a really bad idea).

That became my favorite outfit—and I think the mountain lion came to symbolize, for young Travis Macy, the courage and toughness of my dad.

That courage and toughness was not limited to running and biking—and it extended to my mom as well.

Mace and Pam had been in the long run of life together since they started dating in high school in their hometown of Livonia, Michigan. They both went to Michigan State, and Dad went on to law school at the University of Detroit, graduating in 1980. After he graduated, they moved out to Colorado. They'd been looking for a place in Denver, but one weekend they stumbled across Evergreen while the town was having its annual rodeo. Something about it just captured my parents' imagination—Dad's especially—and they decided that's where they would put down roots in the Great American West.

It takes years to get established as an attorney in another state, and Dad wasn't quite there yet. To help make ends meet, he took a weekend job as a window washer to make a few extra bucks. How he managed to find the time to ride with me, do his own training, *and* wash windows on the weekends is still a mystery to me—but, hey, I guess it's another part of that "it's all good mental training": if you want it, you'll find a way to make it happen.

There was another dynamic at play for the Macy family in 1988: as a parent now myself, I can only imagine how it must have added to the already stressful life of a young family that was struggling financially.

My mom's liver was failing.

Pam Macy first learned that she had abnormal liver function when she had to take a premarital blood test before tying the knot with Mace in 1977. She recalls it as a "big surprise, but not too concerning." The diagnosis was autoimmune hepatitis . . . essentially, inflammation without a known cause.

When they were ready to have kids, Mom's doctors warned her it would be high risk. But while I was a bit of a runt—4 pounds, 13 ounces—I was healthy. Two years later, my parents adopted my sister from Korea. From then on, Mom says, the way they dealt with her illness was to take all the recommended meds, get regular checkups, "and then forget about it."

This is what she had pretty much done for a few years. But in early 1988, her levels started rising again. We didn't know at the time that it would lead to a liver transplant two years later—but still, I'm sure it was in the back of both Mom's and Dad's minds as we drove to Leadville. Of course, we kids were too young to know anything about it. I remember thinking that the coolest thing about Leadville was all these guys walking around with cowboy hats. We had some of that in Evergreen, but this was *real* Wild West territory.

Leadville is today a legendary name among runners and endurance athletes, but its history goes back to just before the Civil War, when a prospector discovered gold in them thar hills. The Leadville area turned out to be one of the richest mineral deposits in the West, and vast fortunes were made here. In the late 1880s, Leadville was the quintessential boom town, attracting the likes of Doc Holliday, Jesse James, and Buffalo Bill. There were gunfights and stagecoach robberies here; there were, no doubt, fancy saloons with pianos tinkling and hard-edged men playing cards; opera houses and houses of ill repute, and everything else you would imagine an Old West town would have had.

A century later, that had all changed. The Climax Mine, for years the economic mainstay of the town and at times the world's leading supplier of molybdenum (an element primarily used in the production of steel), had closed unexpectedly in the early 1980s, and nearly everyone in town was out of work. The whole region was on the brink of economic collapse.

One of the mine's employees was a guy name Ken Chlouber. An Oklahoma native, Chlouber was a rough, tough hombre who, had he been there in the 1880s, would have probably been the sheriff who didn't take any shit. He was also involved in town government, and he decided to try and come up with a way to save his adopted community, where the unemployment rate had soared to 90 percent in the wake of the closure. He heard about the Western States 100, a famous and already well-established ultramarathon in California, and thought that a similar race in Leadville might work, in part because anyone running 100 miles would need to stay overnight, thus providing a boost to the tourism industry. Others thought that anyone running 100 miles in Leadville might need to take advantage of another facility: the local morgue or funeral home. In a June 2014 profile of Chlouber in *Trail*

Runner magazine, writer Garrett Graubins related an anecdote about a local physician who, in a town meeting, objected strenuously to the plans for the new race, saying that having people come in and try and run 100 miles at Leadville's altitude would kill them.

Chlouber dismissed the warning—probably with an expletive directed at the physician—and the first Leadville 100 was held in 1983. All 45 competitors survived. Very quickly, Leadville became a bucket-list race for adventure-minded runners around the country. Although recently there have been concerns about overcrowded fields as the race population has soared (to 1,200 in 2013), it remains one of the most prestigious events in ultradistance running. The reason, in large part, is Chlouber himself. Some find Ken, who is now 75, to be a bit rough around the edges, but he and cofounder Merilee Maupin are still involved with the race, cheering for runners at the start and hugging them when they finish. They've been an inspiration to me, Dad, and thousands of others since that day in 1988.

There was a real family atmosphere at the early Leadville 100s, with everyone out there helping and pulling for each other. Ken's pre-race message, delivered to the racers and their families in the old gym on Sixth Street, was always the same: "You're better than you think you are. You can do more than you think you can. Commit not to quit."

I was listening. Ken was right. I saw it with my own eyes that day, and the lesson—one of the most important in the Ultra Mindset—has stayed with me for over 25 years.

True to its Wild West heritage, Leadville starts with a shotgun blast at 4:00 a.m. I remember being sleepy and cold in the predawn hours that morning, but that loud "bang" woke me up! After that, I mostly remember being energized, curious, excited for Dad, and feeling alive. We watched the start and then went to a coffee shop with Mom and her younger brother, Brian—known to all of us as Uncle B—for breakfast.

I could hardly finish my bear-claw-shaped donut, I was so excited about Dad running in this really cool race. Had I been older and understood a little more about his preparations for it—or lack thereof—I would have totally lost my appetite.

Training for a 100-mile race usually involves starting with a marathon, then building up to what we call the "entry level" ultradistance: 50K (31 miles). From there, you do a 50-miler, maybe two. Races of this kind of distance have to be spaced out over many months, meaning that a smart, safe buildup to a 100-miler is usually a multiyear project.

And yes, crazy as it sounds, there is such a thing as a rational training program for a 100-mile race. Dad's was not that. He had finished the Ironman two years earlier, and that's definitely a significant undertaking. But swimming, biking, and running, even over Ironman distances, doesn't pound the body the way running 100 miles does. Also, the time frame of the Ironman and the 100-miler is completely different: Consider that the former has a 17-hour cutoff. In the Leadville 100, you had to finish in 30 hours to be officially scored.

Running the whole 100 at above 10,000 feet makes for an entirely new game as well.

It wasn't only his insufficient training that put Dad behind the Leadville eight-ball: neither he nor many other people at the time knew much about gear, nutrition, hydration, and pacing for ultradistances. When I do a race like the one in Val d'Isère, I can lace up a pair of Hoka One Ones, a super-cushioned shoe specially designed for ultrarunners, and know that the impact force of countless foot strikes is minimized. I have a special carbohydrate drink, Vitargo, which keeps me from bonking without bloating. I have an Ultimate Direction backpack that feels as soft and light as a cloud on my back; electrolyte pills to stave off dehydration; clothing made of technical fibers to eliminate chafing and swelling; a GPS watch to show me how fast I'm going and how far I've gone; not to mention bright Ay Up lights to see the trail at night.

Dad had none of this. He ran in plain old road running shoes, wore his running shorts and cotton t-shirt, and drank mostly water and Gatorade. The flashlight he had been told to bring along had been purchased at a 7-Eleven on the way to Leadville, and it was better suited for poking around in a dark basement than for lugging 100 miles through the Colorado Rockies.

But he did have something else: grit.

Did Dad's inexperience hurt him in the race? Heck, yeah.

Did Dad's mental training save him? Hell yes it did!

We learned that at the end. At the halfway point, in a little ghost town called Winfield at the bottom of a deep valley surrounded by monumental snow-peaked mountains, Dad was feeling okay. He saw us and decided to have an impromptu little picnic with the family. In retrospect, maybe this suggests that he wasn't thinking clearly. (Trust me, having a picnic in the middle of a 100-mile race is not a suggested race strategy.) Nonetheless, there we were rolling out a blanket and sitting around munching on cheese quesadillas and fruit salad. I remember it was a beautiful mountain afternoon, sunny, warm, and clear.

At his first Leadville 100 in 1988, Dad stopped for a picnic with Mom, Katelyn, and me at the Winfield ghost town at 50 miles. CREDIT: MACY FAMILY

Dad talked animatedly about his race. He had covered 50 miles in 12 hours—50 miles!—and he was confident he could do the second half in about the same time, so there was no need to worry about the 30-hour cutoff. "I feel a lot better than I thought I would," he said, cheerfully.

We finished eating, and off he ran, turning and waving before he disappeared down the wooded trail.

As you can guess, that was the beginning of the end. Things began to fall apart soon after, and they got really bad when Dad began retracing his path to Leadville with a nearly 3,000-foot-high climb back up Hope Pass. By the time he reached the small town of Twin Lakes on the other side of Hope Pass at mile 60, Dad was a shuffling, shaky compendium of overuse injuries. His quadriceps and hamstrings were so tight he could barely move. His feet hurt—he would later be diagnosed with two stress fractures in the metatarsals of both his left and right feet. He was puking from dehydration. His 7-Eleven flashlight burned out a couple of hours after sundown, and he soon found himself feeling his way through the darkness along rocky trails in the woods.

Still, at some point he must have realized amid his largely incoherent thoughts that he was in danger of missing the 30-hour Leadville cutoff. So he hunkered down and somehow summoned the strength to continue.

Did he tell himself what he told me during our Saturday bike rides together? ("Commit to it.")

Did he recycle the inspirational words of Ken Chlouber? ("You can do more than you think you can. . . . Success means never giving up.")

Did he really manage to convince himself that this was "all good mental training"? Or that the mental training he had forged in shorter races could help him overcome this? Or that, given what Mom was going through with her illness at the time, this was nothing?

Years later, when I asked him, he admitted that he'd blocked out a lot from that first race. But he remembers enough about that crucible of pain to know that some kind of spark, some kind of attitude, some kind of mindset . . . an Ultra Mindset . . . kicked in, and took over, out there in the darkness on the grueling climb to Hope Pass.

"As I was on my knees dry heaving," Dad recalls, "it really did seem impossible, but I told myself I would make it as long as I just kept moving. And as long as I kept moving, I kept believing it *was* possible."

Back near the finish line in Leadville, we waited. And waited. And waited. (Most of my memories of the Leadville 100 as a kid involve waiting. Maybe that's one reason I usually try to finish quickly for my own kids when I do Leadville and other ultras!)

Finally, Dad surfaced at the edge of what locals call "The Boulevard," a 2-mile stretch of dirt that brings runners, finally, to the outskirts of Leadville itself. He was clearly in distress, and I can still remember the glazed look in his eyes. It scared me. The time was nearly 10 a.m. of his second day of running. We had checked in at a local hotel, watched TV, slept a bit, and then gone back out on the course at about 4:00 a.m. This was now Dad's second day of running. He had been out there the entire time, working through this self-imposed pain and suffering.

Yet when we saw him emerge the next morning, his broken body, like those of other Leadville finishers then and now, somehow continued to surge forward, even though it clearly should have been lying horizontally somewhere, possibly a hospital bed. In the background, the Rocky Mountains loomed, including the race's high point on Hope Pass. As he came up Sixth Street, he was getting dangerously close to the 10 a.m. cutoff. His gaze, as the clock ticked, was fixed on the finish banner behind where we were standing. His eyes were bloodshot and sleep-deprived, yet somehow full of life and energy. Exhausted beyond comprehension, he could hardly speak but managed a sincere smile for his children. We ran out to hold his hand while he shuffled the final 20 meters of red carpet to the finish.

He had finished dead last.

That didn't matter. Neither did his time: 29 hours, 56 minutes, just 4 minutes off the cutoff, and at that point the closest finish to the cutoff in Leadville history.

The fact was that my dad had finished the Leadville 100—a 100-mile race!

Dad was Superman, and despite the apparent insanity of it all, I wanted to be just like him.

Mace would go on to finish Leadville four more times, earning the prestigious, gaudy belt buckle earned by racers who cross the line in less than 25 hours. More important, he finished strong in each of the next four attempts. He went in prepared and never made the mistake of underestimating the distance again. And Dad's ultra-endurance career began to expand beyond Leadville . . . way beyond. He ran up and down Pikes Peak four times in the Pikes Peak Quad, a race that involved over 100 miles of running and a gain of some 31,000 vertical feet. He finished both the Marathon des Sables, a multiday ultradistance race that crosses over 150 miles in the Sahara Desert, and the Badwater Ultramarathon, often considered the hardest single-day running race and, as it starts in Death Valley, definitely the hottest. On the other end of the temperature spectrum, Dad has also won the Iditashoe, a 100-mile snowshoeing race in Alaska on the Iditarod trail, three times. He even did the epic Eco-Challenge—the seminal adventure race, which was broadcast on the Discovery Channel in the 1990s. (The producer was Mark Burnett, who would subsequently take the idea and develop it into one of the first major network reality shows, *Survivor*.) Dad was one of the few competitors to complete eight Eco-Challenges, which were weeklong races held in some of the most challenging terrain the globe has to offer.

In sum, my dad became a world-class endurance athlete. I became a high-school cross-country runner of no great distinction. Still, I had sucked enough wind during our team training runs in Evergreen to have a small sense of the kind of pain Dad must have endured in

Dad's enthusiasm, energy, and grit tend to make the people around him better. I know that's been the case with me, and it was also true in team races like the Eco-Challenge. His team, the Stray Dogs, never won the Eco, but they never quit either. CREDIT: TIM HOLMSTROM

Leadville in 1988. Ten years after that race, I asked him about it. Was it just a bad memory he tried to blot out? Looking back, did he laugh about it or cringe? Was he embarrassed at himself for having taken on a challenge he was so unprepared for?

He looked at me almost incredulously. "Embarrassed?" he said. "Bud, you must have forgotten what I used to tell you on our rides when you were a little kid."

I admitted that I had forgotten.

"It's all good mental training," he said. "You trying to get your little bike up the hills, me trying to get my body across that finish line. It's all good mental training."

Ultra Mindset 1: It's All Good Mental Training

DAD WAS RIGHT. IT REALLY IS ALL GOOD MENTAL TRAINING.

The idea here is that challenges are part of life. Viewing them as positive, even essential, instruments of "mental training" can build, pebble by pebble, a mountain of inner resilience that will allow you to complete *anything* to which you deeply commit.

These challenges and this mental training, moreover, when experienced through pursuits of choice, generate an incredible well of resolve that allows us all to persevere through the truly challenging, mandatory bouts of suffering dished out by life. So maybe Dad's completion of that first Leadville 100 gave him the mental fortitude to persevere during my mother's illness while trying to raise two small children and build his career.

What do you choose to pursue? For my dad and me, it happens to be things like running 100 miles or competing in adventure races where we go for a week without really sleeping. But yours can be whatever you like to do, or feel intrigued by or compelled to do. Many people find that endurance challenges—whether it's a 5-mile hike or their first 5K race—are an available but challenging goal, and I suspect that's one reason that running, walking, bicycling, and triathlon are so popular today. They offer a reasonable chance of completion, provided you prepare properly; they can be pursued without interfering too much with the rest of your life (get up early and go for a walk!); and they can be done, at least at the beginning levels, without too great an expenditure of time or money.

In the context of the Ultra Mindset, such goals, such events, help forge the mental toughness that can carry you through the real challenges of life: the ones involving family, career, illness, aging parents, finances, what have you—the challenges you didn't choose, but trained for by pursuing the ones you did.

Let me now tweak the meaning of this principle slightly:

It's all good: mental training.

With the addition of that colon, indicating a pause and so much more, we have slightly altered, or perhaps amplified upon, the meaning of the phrase; and in doing so, we are describing the purpose of this text. The positive aphorism, *it's all good*, provides a foundation for the intent of the Ultra Mindset principles I will explain, tried and true from the world of ultra-endurance racing at the elite level.

I like to think that, taken as a whole, such principles, and the stories that prove their worth, provide a sort of applied course in *mental training, one that can be utilized for work, family, athletics, and life.* The Ultra Mindset is not just for ultra athletes. It's for people who want to improve themselves and their lives, and not just in a quick-fix manner, but for the long haul.

Take what works for you, apply it to your own life, commit to something big, achieve peak performance, and come out on the other side with a winning outlook that allows you to do even more next time.

Let's start with this principle of mental training. My advice is to think about training your mental toughness like you would train a muscle. Or, better yet, like you would train a system—heart and lungs, your cardiovascular system—to work together. To get them ready for a task or event, you would practice in intentional ways and undergo simulations to bring them closer to readiness for the final test. Mental training happens the same way. In her 2010 book *Succeed: How We Can Reach Our Goals*, research psychologist Heidi Grant Halvorson, PhD, identifies self-control as a foundational element of reaching success. Attaining a goal, at the most fundamental level, essentially requires doing, in a given moment, what you often don't feel like doing, or feels like you are not capable of doing. That's where training in self-control kicks in. When I have already run 60 miles and have 40 more to go, do I *feel* like running 40 more? I love running, but of course I don't feel like running 40 more miles after running 60! No one does. However, I have reached the point where my self-control is such that, unless I'm suffering a serious physical injury that prevents me from taking a step, I know I'm not going to stop; I know I'm going to continue on for 40 miles, come hell or high water.

I often meet people, healthy people, who tell me they wish they "could" run, wish they "could" bike, wish they "could" get in shape. They wish they had the discipline or self-control needed. They act as if you are either born with this mysterious gift of willpower or not. The latest research on the subject supports the idea that self-control really can be developed and trained, just like you can train your muscles or your memory.

There's a corollary to this idea that Dr. Steven Jonas, MD, a now-retired professor of preventive medicine at Stony Brook University in New York and an accomplished (and still active) triathlete, often uses. "There are no bad experiences," says Dr. Jonas, author of the best-selling tri-training book *Triathlon for Ordinary Mortals*.

By that, he means that in every experience, we can learn something. In every setback, there is wisdom to be found. There are lessons to be learned and applied that can take us to a better place or advance us toward a goal.

So you tried going on a diet and couldn't stick with it? So you invested in a new business and it failed? So the relationship that you thought was "the one" fell apart?

I sympathize, and there's no way that I'm going to tell you that any of those are "good." But on the flip side, I will tell you—and there are plenty of relevant personal and historical examples to choose from—that individuals who went through those experiences, by and large, came out better, stronger, tougher, particularly if they tried to use that setback as a way to learn more about themselves and to avoid repeating mistakes.

Another way of saying that: it's all good mental training.

Reappraising Your Situation

Here's yet another way of looking at mental training that is drawn from cognitive psychology. It's the concept of "cognitive reappraisal." As the name suggests, this is a strategy that involves reframing, or reinterpreting, a situation. The brain gives a new meaning to a situation and responds accordingly. To put it into practical terms, when you're doing something you don't like, instead of thinking about how much it sucks, reappraise it. Say to yourself, "This is good mental training. . . .

It will make me stronger, more resilient, and more prepared to take on other challenges in my life."

The situation doesn't have to be mile 75 in a 100-mile race, either (since that's a situation very few individuals are ever in). Here are several everyday examples of how cognitive reappraisal can reset you from an Unhappy/this-sucks mindset to an Ultra Mindset.

▸ It's finals week, and you know you need to put in a few hours of studying each night in addition to attending class, working your part-time job, exercising, and pursuing that cute girl/guy whose phone number you got. "Why do I have to take this class? . . . The professor's boring. . . . I'd much rather be with my new friend than studying for this." That's what you may be telling yourself. Time for a reappraisal: "This class is one of the last steps toward me getting my degree. I can see the light at the end of the tunnel. Just a little more focused effort and I'll be able to pass this final, and I'm done with it. Structuring these nightly study sessions . . . 60–90 minutes each night . . . is also a good way to learn how to budget my time. *It's all good mental training.*"

▸ Your baby is teething, and your spouse is about to go away on a business trip. You have a big presentation the day after tomorrow, and you know you'll be up at least five times tonight to care for your child. You won't sleep much, and you've got to have your "A" game for the presentation. The Unhappy/this-sucks mindset says: "Why does he have to be away now? Why does she have to be teething now? I wish she was older . . . and I'm beginning to wonder if this parenthood thing was a good idea." The Ultra Mindset says: "With a little preparation, we can do this. Let's rehearse the presentation for an hour tonight, and try to get a good night's sleep. Then tomorrow, when we're on our own with the baby, we'll be rested and halfway there with the presentation, so the pressure will be off a little. It's a challenge, and *it's all good mental training.*"

▸ Your boss has just handed you—for the third time in three weeks—a copy of the report you have worked so very hard on. It's covered in red, and you have to revise it yet again. You know the work is excellent, but your boss sees it another way. Since she's in charge (at least for now), you know your only choice is to put in the time to revise the report to her liking. The Unhappy/this-sucks mindset pouts and grumbles about how she got to be in charge in the first place. The Ultra Mindset figures out the most time-efficient way to get the revisions done, thinks that maybe it's time to get a little more aggressive with the job hunting, and forges ahead with the assignment. Why? Because . . . all together now . . . *It's all good mental training.*

▸ You don't like to exercise because walking, running, biking, and lifting hurt so much. You know, though, that sticking to your commitment to exercise three times each week will make you healthier, more energetic, and more confident in yourself. When the alarm wakes you up at 6 a.m. for your morning workout, you begin to weaken. "We're not getting anywhere with this," says the Unhappy/this-sucks mindset. "Why bother?" The Ultra Mindset says: "We've come this far, let's keep it up. We'll feel great after we're done, and oh, by the way, . . . *it's all good mental training.*" The Ultra Mindset is right: as you begin the last mile of your 3-mile walk (or the last set of your weight-training circuit in the gym), the sun is rising, and you pick up the pace. You feel energized, refreshed, like you can take on anything. Is this that runner's high you've heard about, you wonder? Possibly, but it's most certainly the Ultra Mindset. And let me tell you, that's some powerful medicine.

Get REAL About the Ultra Mindset

For each of our ultra principles, or "Mindsets," some suggested activities—and a little inspiration—are provided. There are three components:

▸ *Reflection:* This will be a self-assessment, some sort of written exercise that will allow you to think about how to apply that specific Mindset to your own life and your own issues, goals, and challenges.

▸ *Activity:* This will be a physical activity, a workout specifically geared toward applying the Mindset. Here, I'll tell you a little about some of my workouts, but don't worry—I'm not saying you need to be doing ultramarathons, or even running, to get the benefit. The activities are designed to suit every fitness level. Everyone should be engaged in regular physical activity.

▸ *Learn from others:* Here, in short "case studies," other champion endurance athletes talk about the Ultra Mindset in action and how these principles have helped them in both their personal and competitive lives.

Put the boldfaced letters of those three components together—Reflections, Activity, and Learning—and you've got the REAL Ultra Mindset. Basically, it's a way for you to tailor these Mindsets to your situation, to practice them, and to be inspired by the examples of others.

So let's get REAL, with our first mindset! *It's all good mental training.*

Mindset 1 REFLECTION

You just read several examples of how various situations in life can be reframed, using the Ultra Mindset, and applied as good mental training. Now it's your turn: List the three biggest challenges or concerns in your life right now. Write down what's making you angry or anxious about each one. Then, rewrite each with an Ultra Mindset approach. For each of your three concerns, reappraise. Write your response, and start each with the words, "It's all good mental training because . . ." This will force you to reappraise the situation and reframe it into a challenge. And you can conclude each with some action steps. Start your conclusion with "I will meet the challenge by . . ." and then list two or three logical next steps.

Mindset 1 ACTIVITY: Make Yourself (Un)comfortable!

Running in extreme heat when you're not acclimated is not comfortable, and can even be dangerous. Here's how competitive ultradistance runners prepare themselves for the heat. If you've got a "hot" race coming up—or if you are just looking for a challenge—you can apply the same principle and use it as an opportunity for practicing the mantra *It's all good mental training*.

How the pros do it: Running in place for an hour in the sauna is a close simulation to, for example, the Badwater Ultramarathon in Death Valley, California, where temperatures soar to over 100°F. My dad and his buddy, the accomplished ultrarunner Marshall Ulrich, did this, and so have I. Another Badwater competitor, who lived in a cold climate, ran on a treadmill in his basement with the exhaust hose from his basement dryer pointed directly at him. In a similar vein, but the opposite climate conditions, Mike Pierce, a runner from San Diego, trained to race a marathon in Antarctica by running in circles in a huge meat locker near his home. On race day, like my dad, Marshall, and the others, "Antarctic Mike," as he now calls himself, was well acclimated for the below-zero conditions of the Last Continent. Pretty impressive for a guy from Southern California!

How you can do it: Besides training specifically for the conditions of their events, what these athletes were also doing was putting themselves in uncomfortable situations. That's what mental training is all about. We're not saying you should run in place in a sauna, rearrange your washer/dryer setup, or go find the nearest meat locker. But you can challenge yourself. Here are a few ways you can add a little discomfort to your life (in order to reap the rewards):

▸ Get up a half hour early at least once a week for the next six weeks, and use that time to exercise (you may find that you actually like it!).

▸ Look for a hill on or near your walking or running route—and next time you're out for a walk or a jog, don't avoid it: attack it!

▸ Before your next gym workout, make a list of the machines or movements you rarely do. Chances are, you'll see that those are exercises working body parts you don't like working—which in turn suggests that they probably need working the most. So devote one workout every two weeks to these poor old neglected muscles. Put together a workout of movements—whether machines, free weights, or your own bodyweight—that you rarely do. Check with a trainer or online to make sure you're doing the exercises properly.

▸ During your regular workout on the elliptical machine, the treadmill, or the stationary bike, set the level higher, by one: Stay there for 3 minutes, and then resume your normal intensity. Try building up to 3 on and 3 off for an entire workout.

You will accrue many physiological benefits from ratcheting up the intensity (carefully and gradually) in your workouts. But in terms of this book, the most important benefit you'll get is not in your heart, it's in your head: this is good mental training, and it builds a reservoir of confidence for you that you can apply in other aspects of life.

Mindset 1 LEARN

Danelle Ballengee

RACING LIFE

In the 1990s and early 2000s, Danelle, who also happens to be from my small town of Evergreen, ruled the trail both domestically and abroad, whether she was running, snowshoeing, or doing triathlon or adventure racing. She won 103 snowshoe races, 2 Adventure Racing World Championships, 3 Primal Quest Adventure Races, 9 Mt. Taylor Quadrathlons, 4 Pikes Peak Marathons, and enough other races to fill this book. In 2000, she climbed all 55 of Colorado's 14,000-foot peaks. In 14 days. When I started adventure racing with Nellie in 2004, I couldn't believe how many races she did every year—and the fact that she won almost every single one of them!

REAL LIFE

While Nellie is known widely for a near-death fall during a run from a cliff outside of Moab, Utah, in December 2006, her defining traits are that she is a good person, a loyal friend, a hardworking business owner, and a committed and involved mother of two young children. Still, I think you'll agree, when you read her account of it, that her near-death story is pretty remarkable. Years of mental training clearly allowed her to survive two sub-freezing nights in the desert with internal bleeding and a shattered pelvis, but what I believe to be even more significant is the way her mental training for and within racing prepared her for parenting, work, and other aspects of life. Nellie and her husband, BC, run Milt's Stop and Eat at the base of the Slickrock Trail in Moab. You may want to stop after your next big ride there, just to see in person a woman who has accomplished and survived what she has—and to take down some tasty calories and a thick milkshake!

DANELLE'S THOUGHTS ON APPLYING MENTAL TRAINING

It wasn't until after I turned 40—after a successful endurance-racing career, a near-death accident, and two kids later—that I looked back on my life and realized the value of my inherent positive mindset. This optimistic attitude is not only important to live a more fulfilling life, but in my case it actually saved my life in a "should be death" experience.

For me, the feeling of achievement of crossing the line, making the summit, or achieving whatever goal I set far surpasses the obstacles one must overcome along the way; and for me these obstacles were not stopping blocks, but rather welcoming challenges that made achieving the goal even sweeter. Having grown up competing in endurance events, this is what I grew to know. Perhaps the flow of positive endorphins received from exercise shaped my brain to give me the "never give up" attitude. Due to the hard efforts, at times the smile was missing from my face, but within I had a feeling of "this is awesome"—I was doing my best and truly "living" life. I remember a few times when my attitude turned south, and these memories haunt me as if I committed a crime. I still feel guilty for my moments of negativity.

Some would say it's only theory that positive attitude equals positive results, but I believe it's true. I believe that a positive mind can physically adapt to allow almost superhuman capabilities in times of need. For me this was proven between December 13 and December 15 of 2006. I survived sub-freezing temperatures (in my jogging outfit) and extreme internal bleeding due to a shattered pelvis after a 60-foot fall. Why? I stayed positive. I fought away death. Doctors claim most people die from internal bleeding or hypothermia alone in a quarter of the time that I was out there. Once I was rescued, I was told I might not walk again. But 5 months later, just 2 months out of a wheelchair, I competed a 12-hour adventure race.

I was alive, so why not?

As I grow older, my competitive drive in racing has lessened as I have developed more patience and become calmer through raising kids and running a business, but similarly, perhaps even more so, I find my positive attitude is a key to my happiness. Every day I realize how lucky I am to be alive and to be able to experience the ups and downs that life throws at us. I find a sense of achievement in seeing the happiness in my kids and seeing our business succeed. And my drive to explore the outdoors and conquer the miles in new places is still strong and gives me a goal to look forward to. I realize that there is positive to be found so long as one sets a goal that is achievable. That goal might be taking the first step out of a wheelchair. Or it may mean skipping all other plans to tend to a sick child. Or it may mean making the summit of a peak . . . in record time!

—Nellie

Be a Wannabe

LIKE MANY BOYS GROWING UP IN THE EARLY 1990S, I wanted to be like the athletes I watched on TV. Guys like Michael "Air" Jordan, "Neon" Deion Sanders, and Bo "Knows" Jackson were obvious choices—in part because they had such memorable nicknames.

My neighborhood buddies and I spent day after day at Wilmot Elementary pretending to be those superstars on the playground. Most kids stuck to the prominent pro sports in picking their idols, gazing out the Wilmot windows at the basketball court and baseball field in anticipation of recess, when they, too, could "Be Like Mike" (or imagine they were).

I, on the other hand, had another set of athletic heroes as well. I remember with great clarity looking out the window from Mr. Philippe's fifth-grade classroom at nearby Bear Mountain, one of the many peaks in Evergreen, wondering how steep the roads there were, how sharp the switchbacks could be, and whether Greg LeMond, Bernard Hinault, Miguel Indurain, or Dad would win in a time trial to the top.

From Dad and the copies of *UltraRunning Magazine* he left lying around the house, I learned about guys like Marshall Ulrich, who could run for days through the desert and won the Badwater Ultramarathon year after year; Tom Sobal, a Colorado legend who won hundreds (yes, literally, hundreds) of mountain running and snowshoeing races; and Matt Carpenter, who ran up and down Pikes Peak and other mountains in record time before setting a Leadville 100 mark that still inspires awe in endurance athletes.

I dreamt about the Kiwi and Aussie adventure racers: John Howard was both a window cleaner by trade and also the best navigator in the world; John Jacoby was a beast of a man who could paddle through anything and run a sub-3:00 marathon even though he was oversized and awkward on his feet; Neil Jones was a hard-ass hunter of feral pigs in the New Zealand bush who won more races than anyone simply because he was so damn tough.

Such characters from the remote fringes of organized sport entered my mind via personal experience and stories from Dad, or an occasional broadcast on some obscure cable channel (we moved to a slightly less remote neighborhood when I was 10, and finally had more than four choices of what to watch on TV). These athletes permeated my consciousness, and I pretended to be like them while mountain biking and running in the woods around Evergreen.

When I entered Evergreen High School in 1997, I—like most of the other freshman athletes—tried out for the soccer, track, and basketball teams. We watched the older boys and tried to emulate some of them. While most of my friends wanted to be like the high scorers—the running backs, the strikers, the point guards—I gravitated toward the guys who kept a spot on the team by playing hard and leading by example in practice. These were the guys who threw themselves onto the court to dive for loose balls, or threw the blocks that sprang the stars for touchdowns.

I did become, perhaps not surprisingly, a distance runner, although distance in high school track at that time was just 2 miles. My time, 9:49 for that event, was good enough to make All-State (as I also did in cross-country), but nothing that was going to attract major college coaches. Yet, the sport that really left an impact on me was basketball. At 5'10" and 135 lbs., I was a skinny kid with very little talent. I shot so poorly that one team decided they would double-team our best guy and simply let me roam the court. But I played hard, and I wasn't afraid of anyone. Since I clearly wasn't going to do much on offense, my role was to shut down the other team's best guy, and in one key game I matched up against a 6'6," 200-pound ringer who would go on to become a college star. Right off the bat, he hit three 3-pointers in my face, and our coach, Mr. Haebe, called a time-out.

Coach Scott Haebe was—and is—a legendary and passionate history teacher, too, and in his basketball coaching and history classes he has been a mentor for generations of young men and women who grew up in Evergreen. Before returning to Colorado to start a family and become a high school teacher and coach, he had spent a few years playing professional ball in Austria, where he met his wife, Klaudia. Before that, he was a talented basketball player for Adams State College in Alamosa, Colorado. At the time of this time-out, he was 41 years old and a seasoned coach, having lead Evergreen's team for ten years.

Coach Haebe was the kind of guy who worked hard in everything he did. He was the kind of guy who inspired you to play even harder. He was the kind of guy who, at times, got pretty fired up and in your face.

This was one of those times.

"Travis! You're killing us!" Coach's yell echoed through the silent gym. I could feel the saliva spray on my face.

"Damn it, Coach! I know it!" I yelled right back (and, truth be told, the words that actually came out of my mouth were a bit stronger than "damn").

Everyone on the bench sat up straight. I saw a couple of my teammates look at each other wide-eyed with shock; as if to say, *"Did we just hear that right? Did Macy . . . quiet, polite Macy . . . just yell . . . curse, even! . . . at Coach Haebe?"*

Maybe it was teenage hubris, or maybe it was having an ego and using it effectively. Or maybe I was just tired of being embarrassed by the big guy from the other team. Whatever the case, Coach actually seemed to like my reaction. He knew that I had to be pretty angry to say what I said, and he could sense I was even more upset and passionate about the situation than he was. He just nodded and put me right back in. In the "Hoosiers" version of this little story, I would have shut down the big guy on the other team completely. But this is real life, and while I did get in his face a few times, disrupting his game just enough to have him give me some dirty looks, he continued to score. What I really accomplished was getting my teammates fired up. They figured if modest Macy could get angry and step up his game, so could they. We came away with the win, and although the story in the school paper was about the guys who scored the baskets, I know that I played a key role in my own quiet—well, maybe on that day, not so quiet—way.

Coach Haebe still tells this story to his current high-school players. He's helping them develop mental toughness and passion by using me—a kid who wasn't really very "good" at basketball, but somehow found a way to contribute to the team and make his teammates play harder—as an example. It's nice to know that they might want to be a bit like me in that way.

I am deeply grateful for what I learned from playing basketball under that man. To this day, when I'm struggling through the middle third of an ultra run, I can hear Haebe's directions to us during the

I was an All-State runner and 11-time letterman at Evergreen High School. I competed in cross-country and soccer in the fall, basketball in the winter, and track in the spring. Academically, my work ethic earned me a place as valedictorian and student body co-president. But Coach Haebe's basketball program, which was an extended exercise in mental toughness, is what really left a mark on me.
CREDIT: MACY FAMILY

10 x 200–meter running workout during our preseason Hell Week: "Anyone can go hard on the last sprint of the workout," he'd say about halfway through. "If you're tough, you'll go hard on each and every one."

A few days after I graduated from high school in 2001, Dad and I flew to Anchorage, Alaska, where we rented a pickup truck with an old camper on top. Our only agenda for the week was to go running, see wild places, catch some fish, and talk about my future. Lying in that camper late at night under the Midnight Sun, I read *Running with the Buffaloes*, Chris Lear's close-up chronicle of a year spent with the distance runners at the University of Colorado at Boulder. I immediately decided that I wanted to be like the walk-ons who became All-Americans through hard work in Coach Mark Wetmore's program. Dad agreed, and we created a plan for my next step in life.

When we got back home, I resumed the window-cleaning job that I'd been doing since I was 16—yes, the same local company Dad had worked for years earlier (nepotism isn't a part of the Ultra Mindset, but it is a part of life!). Window cleaning isn't glamorous, but I could make a decent amount of money by working hard and planning my routes carefully. It also gave me the flexibility to train a lot; I had been accepted to CU and was gearing up for the cross-country tryout just after school started in the fall.

I ran every day that summer, sometimes with other people, but usually (as I do now) alone, because I was putting in miles early in the morning, at lunchtime, or in the evening—or all three. I set up my window-cleaning schedule so I could run with the CU guys on their "unofficial" team runs two mornings each week. We ran the hills around Boulder as well as the flat trails in town and on local roads. Most of all, we ran fast; getting to 6:30 or 7:00 per mile at altitude on easy days was a step up for me at the time and I felt my body respond accordingly. I was getting fitter and stronger.

A week after the fall semester began, the walk-on contenders—athletes who did not already have scholarships or guaranteed spots on the roster—would compete in a special try-out race. The top three would earn a coveted team spot. The rest would walk away.

I was determined to make the team. At around that same time, Mom's health problems had flared up, and I kept her in my mind. As she often does, her quiet, no-complaints attitude inspired me, in this case helping me run one of my best races to date: I was the top walk-on at the tryout, finishing ahead of about ten other guys. I could tell that Coach Wetmore was impressed. He saw how hard I'd worked, and how it paid off. He rewarded me in kind, offering me a spot on the team. I was stoked! Dad was there, and he was stoked, too.

I'd love to tell you I became the next surprise sensation for the CU Buffaloes, showing up from a small town to become an All-American

I read Chris Lear's *Running with the Buffaloes* and was inspired to become one of the walk-on to All-American athletes he talks about in the book. I did make the team, but keeping up with future Olympians in the short, fast races was tough—so was the competitive team social structure that ranked us according to how fast we were. Two years was enough for me, and I moved happily on to triathlon and then adventure racing.
CREDIT: MACY FAMILY

and captain the team. Well, that's not how it worked out. During my two years on the CU cross-country and track teams, I didn't have the talent to hang in practices, in races, or in the social structure of the team, which was also based on one's potential to run in the Olympics (and many of them did—Wetmore is an exceptional coach and has created a solid foundation for many Olympians in his time at CU). I ran 15:52 for 5K, which might be good enough to win the local Turkey Trot, but is nothing worth noting when many of your teammates are breaking 14:00. Two years of running with the Buffs was enough for me.

My moments of glory would come later, often out in the middle of nowhere or late at night, when few people, and certainly not Coach Wetmore, were watching. But my experience running at CU certainly helped me appreciate them more. Looking back, I wouldn't change a thing, and I'm proud that I, too, was able to run with the Buffaloes.

During my junior year at CU, I began thinking again of the Iron-man triathletes I had watched on TV with Dad as a kid, people like Mark Allen and Dave Scott. These guys were legends in the world of endurance sports. Even casual fans knew of their almost superhuman exploits in Kona.

Could I be like them?

I joined the CU Club Triathlon Team to find out. Today, triathlon has become a popular collegiate club sport, and participation in swim-bike-run events by college students has grown dramatically. Back then, it was new, and it was exciting to be a part of a sport that was really taking off. Having been a varsity runner (fifteenth guy on the 15-man team, but I didn't tell them that), I had an ego that at times kept me from contributing what I could have as a team player. I learned to swim (sort of) and did two triathlons, finishing tenth in the 2004 Collegiate National Championship in 1:54 for Olympic distance (1,500-meter swim, 40-kilometer bike, 10-kilometer run).

It's a good thing the swim wasn't any longer or they probably would have had to drag me out of the water before I even got to the bike leg.

Both collegiate running and triathlon were out of the picture for my final year of college, and I shifted my focus to a hot new endurance sport that had already made a big impact on, of all places, national television.

The term "adventure racing" gets thrown around a lot, so I think it's worth clarifying. These days, it seems that any event that involves crawling through mud or climbing over some military-style obstacles is labeled an "adventure" race. While some of those mud runs can be fun, and I think it's great that more people are challenging themselves in new ways, real adventure racing is a distinct genre of endurance sports. It involves the core disciplines of running/trekking, mountain biking, using fixed ropes (rappel, Tyrolean traverse, and more), and paddling (kayaks, rafts, canoes, etc.) as well as navigation with map and compass.

Competitive adventure racers possess a wide range of skills, including rappelling, ascending, and traversing fixed ropes. This rappel into a huge limestone cave in China was a blast! CREDIT: CHINESE MOUNTAINEERING ASSOCIATION

That last part suggests what sets it apart. Nobody needs a navigator in a marathon or a triathlon. Whereas those races typically involve set distances that are consistent from race to race, adventure races throw together disciplines in a helter-skelter format that matches the land and local culture. In addition to the core sports mentioned previously, adventure races also include, from time to time, region-specific events like horseback riding, camel trekking, rock climbing, ziplining, mountaineering, skiing, and the "princess chair" (an event often found in adventure races in China, in which three teammates carry the fourth in a bamboo chair with long handles that looks like something from a Disney movie). Adventure racing is a team sport, and most races involve coed teams of four, racing either nonstop for a week or so (for an "expedition race"), or in stages that involve 8 to 12 hours of racing each day, with a bit of rest in a tent overnight (for a "stage race"). The remote nature, extended time, vast distances, challenging navigation requirements, variety of sports, and sleep deprivation involved make this kind of adventure racing the real deal.

The two original, classic adventure races were the Raid Gauloises and the Eco-Challenge, which helped propel adventure racing to prominence by virtue of its Mark Burnett–produced Discovery Channel exposure in the late 1990s and early 2000s. The Eco-Challenge also inspired Burnett's next big idea—*Survivor*. The castaways-on-an-island series became a huge hit on CBS and helped launch the entire reality television era. Adventure races like the Eco-Challenge are part of the lineage that created the idea of contestants challenging themselves in "real" situations (even if the shows got more and more ridiculous as time went on).

By the time I hit the adventure racing scene, those two races had phased out, but the sport was growing rapidly at the local and national levels, and new international races—like the Raid World Championship, the Primal Quest, the Adventure Racing World Series, and the Adventure Racing World Championship—had become just as competitive as the Raid and Eco-Challenge ever were (none of them were ever as successful on TV with general audiences, though, proving perhaps that in this case, reality TV was more interesting to the average American TV viewer than reality itself!).

Being a wannabe—looking to other athletes whom I could emulate—had worked well for me in the past, and when it came to adventure racing I decided to use that strategy from my days at Wilmot Elementary. Once again, I wanted to be like Mike—but in this case, it was Mike Kloser, the guy who won the Mountain Biking World Championship in 1988, back when Dad and I were out doing our mental training rides around the neighborhood.

In the years since, Kloser had gone on to become America's most successful adventure racer. He featured prominently in the Eco-Challenge broadcasts on the Discovery Channel. Dad had also gotten to know him well, so I grew up watching him race on TV and in person.

Born in 1959, Mike Kloser grew up in Dubuque, Iowa, as one of ten children. He played some pickup games in typical team sports as a kid, but he was never a star athlete in the traditional team sports. Iowa was not a hotbed for outdoor activity, and Mike, feeling the pull toward more adventurous sports, found himself moving as a young man to Vail, Colorado. He began mogul skiing and dirt-bike riding, and soon he and his wife, Emily, were spending summers in Europe so he could compete as a professional mountain biker. By the late 1990s, when his second professional racing career, adventure racing, was born, Kloser had moved beyond pro mountain biking and was working as director of activities at Beaver Creek Resorts. (Mike's and Emily's kids have the Ultra Mindset, too: Christian is a superb mountain biker and Nordic skier, and their daughter, Heidi, represented the United States as a skier at the 2014 Winter Olympics in Sochi.)

Mike Kloser is the only guy I know who actually had his own day. Yes, in recognition of his achievements, Vail, Colorado, held Mike Kloser Day in 1997. How do you get your own day in Vail? You compile a racing resume like this:

▸ Four-time Adventure Racing World Champion
▸ World Mountain Bike Champion
▸ World Long Distance Orienteering Champion
▸ Three-time Eco-Challenge Champion
▸ Five-time Primal Quest Champion
▸ Multiple National Adventure Racing Series Champion
▸ Two-time National Winter Triathlon Champion
▸ Ten-time Steamboat Pentathlon Champion
▸ Three-time Teva Mountain Games Adventure Race Champion
▸ Seven-time Breckenridge Imperial Champion
▸ Three-time Aspen Highlands Inferno Champion

- ▸ Two-time Iditabike Champion
- ▸ Mt. Taylor Quadrathlon Champion
- ▸ Moab 24–Hour Mountain Bike Champion
- ▸ Five-time Elk Mountain Traverse Champion
- ▸ Ultra 100 Mountain Bike Champion
- ▸ Two-time America's Uphill Champion
- ▸ National Off-Road Duathlon Champion
- ▸ Colorado State Snowshoe Champion
- ▸ Dearborn Mogul Skiing Champion
- ▸ Jackson Hole Open Mogul Skiing Champion
- ▸ Mountain Bike Hall of Famer
- ▸ Everest "Adventure Sports" Award Winner
- ▸ *Competitor* Magazine Adventure Athlete of the Year (2001)

Maybe you have, or maybe you haven't, heard of some of these events that Mike has won. That's okay. I can tell you that they all have this in common: they're all long, grueling, difficult challenges, whether contested on tire, ski, or foot. And long, grueling, difficult is where Mike shines.

So, is there anything really special, or unique, or different about Mike that enables him to meet these kinds of challenges? I believe the answer is no. Mike's secret is that he:

(a) works relentlessly hard at *everything* he does; and
(b) *always* shows up, rain or shine.

You know the famous Woody Allen line about success? It's often stated in various ways, and it was originally attributed to something someone heard him say on the set of one of his movies. The actual quote, later confirmed by Allen himself to *New York Times* language columnist William Safire, is that "80 percent of success is showing up."

I don't know if Mike is a Woody Allen fan, but he certainly exemplifies his most famous quote. Kloser is there when you need him; he's there for his teammates, he's there for the big races, and he's there when things happen. As he told a reporter from the *Rocky Mountain News*: "My philosophy is 'Never let the day slip away' or 'Why put off for tomorrow what you can do today?' I like to maximize the time that is available and capitalize on the beauty of each and every day."

While I, too, would love to have a day in my honor, Mike's impressive resume is not why I want to be like him. What I *do* seek to emulate is Mike's work ethic and his ability to hang in there, to be present, to show up.

Being there, in thick and thin, mile after mile: *that's* part of the Ultra Mindset.

▲▲▲

WHEN I WAS IN HIGH SCHOOL, DAD AND I STAYED WITH MIKE AND his family in Vail one evening before our snowshoe race the next day, which Mike would also be doing. As we retired for the night, Mike apologized for some possible noise coming from the bathroom over the next few hours, because he would be tiling the floor. *Wait—it's 10:00 p.m. the night before a race, and you are going to start tiling the bathroom now?* It was classic Kloser: his view is that getting the job done and doing it well trump time, place, and what most people consider to be possible or appropriate. Another way of saying it: you do what you have to do.

When you're racing against Mike Kloser—and I racked up more than enough places behind him or his team over the years to get a firsthand look—he comes across as a relentless, no-holds-barred competitor; someone who does anything possible, within the rules, to win. He comes across as a man with a target on his back, someone

who knows everyone is out to beat him, but still manages to win almost every time.

That's true as well.

Kloser may also seem, at least to his competitors, like someone
who is so single-minded that he would never go out of his way to
help another person; a man to whom the idea of patience, or of
letting anything distract him from his goal of winning, would be
as foreign as the remote places around the world where he often
achieves victory.

This, however, could not be further from the truth.

This is also why I want to be like this Mike. Because he shows up,
every day, with *full presence*, showing his extreme care for his teammates, his indefatigable energy for helping people who need his ex-
pertise, his surprising amount of patience, and his unflagging positive
attitude and enthusiasm.

Ten days before the Adventure Racing World Championship in
2007—the biggest race of the year and one in which Mike planned to
lead his team to the win—Mike took a nasty dive while running the
technical trails outside his house in Vail. His index finger had been
knocked out of its socket, and, as he described it later (no doubt
with characteristic understatement), there was "a good bit of blood
coming out." Never one to miss an opportunity to be productive,
Mike taped some paper towels and a plastic bag on his hand before
heading to work at Beaver Creek Resort, where he chaired a meeting
(probably with his hand raised above his heart). The next stop was
the hospital, where a surgeon righted the injury and stitched him up.
When most people sustain a serious injury, they stay home and heal
for a bit. When Mike was hurt, he promptly got surgery on his finger,
sucked up the lingering pain, and showed up fully present, like he
always does.

Mike's team—minus, perhaps, one fully functioning finger—took
on the best in the world and came out on top. How do you paddle a

kayak with a splint on your hand? I'm not sure, but when you work relentlessly and show up with full presence, I guess you just figure it out.

About such incidents, Mike says, "I always just told myself, 'it could be worse.'" Starting a weeklong race with a lame hand may not have been ideal, but champions don't count on ideal. They suck it up and get out there anyway.

Years of hard work and application of Ultra Mindset principles would bring me, in time, to a level at which racing alongside Kloser as a teammate was a good fit for both of us. Yes, Kloser was in his early fifties by then, but the length of adventure races and the importance of mental toughness in them means that some exceptional older athletes can still run with the young guns. I was going for the win in adventure races in France and China against top international competition—with Mike Kloser on my team!

One race, the Wulong Mountain Quest in China, uses a significant prize purse to draw the best teams in the world. Mike and his team, who had finished in the top three the previous year, were heading back. One teammate from that squad couldn't attend, and they asked me to replace him. Maybe Mike figured that if Travis Macy could be half as good as Mark Macy—whom Kloser knew from the Eco-Challenge—he might be a good sub. Never mind that Mike was old enough to *be* my father. Just to be asked to compete beside him was an honor. The rest of his team was top notch, too, and included (as was mandatory for all the teams) one female, Gretchen Reeves, a successful professional mountain-bike racer, also from Colorado's Vail Valley. Jay Henry was a former National Champion mountain biker and a positive, easy-going presence on the team.

The complex, hectic travel schedule—with gear bags, bikes, paddles, and food packed onto a series of planes, buses, trains, and trucks—that precedes every international adventure race brought us to Chongqing, China. I had never heard of it either, but it's actually a city with 29 million inhabitants. That's more than three times the size

I was happy to be out there racing in China against the best teams in the world. Left to right are Jay Henry, Gretchen Reeves, me, and Mike Kloser. Mike was well into his fifties, but he made great contributions physically and with his leadership style.
CREDIT: CHINESE MOUNTAINEERING ASSOCIATION

of New York City (note to self, pay attention to China). From there, a final bus trip took us an hour into the countryside. The contrast was staggering. The villagers lived off the land in modest dwellings of concrete, sheet metal, and sticks; their lifestyle was very different from that of the booming twenty-first-century metropolis just down the road. For four days, these people cheered and waved at us as we passed their terraced rice paddies and navigated the steep hills, dark forests, deep canyons, and gushing rivers that were also part of the striking landscape in this part of China.

The first day of racing went well. By the second day, we were riding at the front with a couple of other teams. Teammate Jay Henry and I had been working hard on the massive mountain-bike climb, trading off pace-setting while I—the team's navigator—also paid attention to the map and compass, which were held constantly in my line of sight by a bike-specific, rotating map board.

I had spent hours the previous day poring over our maps to make sure we'd take the quickest, most efficient route among the many available on a myriad of logging roads, trails, and foot paths.

Suddenly, a shot rang out. I thought for a second that maybe some testy local farmer didn't get the memo about the race, and thought we were trespassing on his property.

It turned out to be a broken spoke on Gretchen's wheel. Jay, Gretchen, and I were simply happy for a break. Mike, however, sprang into action and rigged up a temporary fix to get us through the stage, the second of five straight days of racing for eight to twelve hours per day.

We finished second that day, returned to a hotel, and spent three or four hours arranging our gear for the next day. It was now late at night, and we had to get up early to race again. Needless to say, most of us were ready to hit the hay.

Not Mike, though. An athlete on another team had a mechanical problem: the hydraulic brake cable on his mountain bike had broken

At this point in our race in China, my teammates paddled a small raft using thin, wooden sticks. They carried all four mountain bikes, and I swam along behind. CREDIT: CHINESE MOUNTAINEERING ASSOCIATION

during that day's stage. A broken brake cable is significant, because riding without brakes is not a good idea. It's also not an easy fix. An experienced bike mechanic in a shop full of the best parts and tools might still need a couple of hours to remove the broken components, install a new cable, fill it with fresh fluid, carefully remove all air bubbles, and calibrate and test the new system. Mike didn't let the late hour, the lack of a bike stand and other tools, his challenging race the next day, any concern about being over 50 when most of his competitors were in their twenties—or the simple fact that he was in the middle of China without a bike mechanic in sight—discourage him as he pitched in to help with the bike-repair effort.

Late that night, the bike was up and running, and the rider was able to complete the remainder of the race.

All this for a guy on another team. The most experienced, most decorated athlete in the entire field was donating hours of time on a bike fix that would in no way help him or his own team. But those of us who know Mike knew that he was simply being Mike. Working relentlessly, showing up, and helping out are just part of why I respect him.

Work hard and relentlessly in everything you do; show up every single day with a positive attitude and your full presence—these are components of the Ultra Mindset that I learned from Mike Kloser, in a foreign city, in the midst of one of the most intense experiences of my life.

And, oh yes, we finished second overall in the race, beaten only by a team of Kiwi juggernauts. That was the last race I did with Mike, but what I learned there sticks with me to this day and proved essential to my team and solo victories on a greater scale later on.

Ultra Mindset 2: Be a Wannabe

WHEN I WAS IN MIDDLE SCHOOL, A WANNABE WAS ABOUT THE WORST thing you could possibly be accused of being. As it turns out, wanting to be like other people is integral to the Ultra Mindset. I'm not saying that you should not be yourself, or that you should try to be *exactly* like someone else, but selecting key role models and working to emulate them in one way or another is absolutely essential to setting big goals, figuring out how to achieve them, and then actually doing it. Looking back, I can now see that my development as an athlete and as a person was integrally related to my natural tendency to emulate what I saw successful people doing: people I had watched on TV and read about, whether Greg LeMond or Mark Allen, as well as people I had come to know personally through my dad, such as Marshall Ulrich and Mike Kloser.

In her book *Mindset*, Stanford University psychologist Carol Dweck sings the praises of the "growth mindset," which, in a nutshell, involves a constant focus on getting better as the key ingredient to success and well-being. This book has made a big difference for me and for many of my students and athletes, and I highly recommend it.

Many of us, Dweck writes, fall into a "fixed mindset" (the opposite of the growth mindset) in one or more areas of life. In a fixed mindset, we constantly judge ourselves, compare ourselves to others, and see any challenge as a test of our fixed—or unchanging—abilities, intelligence, capability, speed, strength, skill, and so on. The growth mindset, on the other hand, recognizes that none of these functions are set in stone, and we can always get better. A given challenge or test—be it a 5K road race or an Ironman triathlon, the ACT or the MCATs, a job interview or parenthood—is no longer a determination of how "good" or "smart" or "talented" we are (and, according to the fixed mindset, always will be). It is merely a snapshot of how well we perform in a given task at a given time. In other words, just because you didn't finish the tri the first time, just because you didn't ace the test or get the job, doesn't mean that you won't perform well in the next challenge, or can't get better through hard work and improving relative weaknesses.

Knowing that we can get better through hard work and effort helps us deal better with failures or setbacks and allows us to see them not as "fixed" events, but as steps in a process of growth—a process that will lead us to eventual mastery, or at least improvement.

Wannabes with a *fixed* mindset look at people they admire and think, "I really want to be like them, but they have got something special and I don't have the same stuff." Fixed mindsetters then feel bad because they have convinced themselves that they don't have what it takes: "I'm not smart enough," "I'm not talented enough," "I'm not attractive enough." Instead of learning from the people they admire, they become jealous, resentful, angry, and upset.

Wannabes with a *growth* mindset, on the other hand, think, "Wow, those people have really worked hard to get to where they're at. I like the way they roll; I like their work ethic; I like the way they go about their business. By watching them continue to succeed, I can learn about the specific actions they take and begin to do the same things myself." Growth mindset wannabes can view the achievements of the people they want to be like as inspirational. So you reframe jealousy and resentment as challenges, aspirations, and motivation; you tell yourself that you can grow, you can change, you can work harder and smarter, and as a result, you can be more like that person in the ways that you admire.

Mindset 2 REFLECTION

If you're like me, some of the people you "wannabe" like are friends, family members, teammates, or professional colleagues. That's only natural, as these are the people you are in a position to observe most closely. Sometimes a bit of jealousy can creep in with a fixed mindset. But instead of harboring grudges or resentment over a sibling or colleague's achievements, try being a wannabe with a growth mindset. Try asking yourself what it is that you can do to achieve similar goals. My prediction is that you will find yourself empowered not only to strive toward your goals more fully, but also to support your friends and family more fully in their own journeys to greatness (which will, in turn, inspire you further).

I know I have found this to be true. You've already met a few people I want to be like in one way or another: my dad, Coach Haebe, Mike Kloser. There are many others.

Select the people you want to be like carefully, and then stalk them. No, not *that* kind of stalking—what I mean is that you should study them, observe them from close up or from afar. Learn about what they do to progress toward the same goals you want to achieve, make time to take them out for coffee or go for a run or a beer together, if possible. In short, be intentional about sucking in their positive influence, almost through osmosis, if you will. Make the most of that goal contagion. I'm telling you, it works for me, and one of the coolest things about it is that is works whether you actually know the person well or not—you don't have to have a champion endurance athlete for a father, like I did, to find role models. They might be coaches, teachers, colleagues, or someone in the local bicycling club. Sometimes you have to intentionally put yourself in the midst of these people (for example, joining that local club, or signing up for one of their classes, or simply seeking them out, via social media, or even better, personal contact) to find them.

Who do you wannabe like? Think about it. I did. My list is shown on pages 70–71. Sorry for the surfeit of superlatives, but hey . . . they're people I admire and aspire to be like.

Now it's your turn! List three people you admire in the table on pages 72–73. To get you started, I'll give you some guidelines. Choose one person you don't know—it could be someone prominent in your field or even famous. Choose one person you do know. And for the third one, I want you to be honest with yourself and choose someone whose achievements you're envious of. Come on, fess up! I know there's someone out there like that for you, as there is for all of us. But by assessing that person objectively for once, you will begin to take on more of a growth mindset—the right kind of wannabe!

Person	Why I Want to Be Like Him or Her
Jeff Jewell Jeff was a world-class athlete "body worker" for me and countless others before taking on a terminal battle with brain cancer that ended a few years ago. Everyone who got a massage from Jeff discovered that his true purpose was to make you believe in yourself and make you a better person.	Jeff's contagious energy for life was unparalleled. He met with clients at his home massage table at 4:00 a.m. and at midnight because he knew he was making a difference and clearly enjoyed doing so.
Philippe Ernewein As director of education at a prestigious private school, Philippe possesses the pedigree of proven leader. More impressive than Philippe's resume, though, is his constant focus on getting *even* better.	He's always reading, thinking, sharing, and teaching. Sometimes you come away from a conversation with someone energized for life and empowered to do anything; this happens every time with Philippe.
Jay Johnson Jay, director of the Boulder Running Camps and a former CU Buffalo star, is one of the best endurance coaches you'll find anywhere. I particularly admire his work ethic, creativity, authenticity, and entrepreneurial presence.	Jay does a great job using media, and I'm constantly trying to learn from him regarding my roles as athlete, coach, and businessman. He's always pulling in literary connections and recommending good books—the English teacher in me really likes that.
Dean Karnazes and Robyn Benincasa Karno and Robyn are listed together because I admire their work as athlete-entrepreneurs. They started with successful careers in ultrarunning and adventure racing, respectively.	They discovered that, through smart, hard work, they could make a difference in people's lives and make money by sharing their experiences and expertise through speaking, workshops, writing, and other endeavors.
Amy, Wyatt, and Lila I really do want to be like my wife and kids. As of this writing, Amy runs a successful private college counseling business at macycollegeconsulting.com, and Wyatt, three, and Lila, one, are happy little kids.	Amy's work ethic and drive to constantly get better keep me on my toes and remind me to do the same. Wyatt's enthusiasm and pursuit of being active just for fun and adventure remind me that—at the core—that's why I run and bike, too. Lila is a lover, and I want to be more affectionate, like her.
Jim Downton Jim is a sociology professor at CU-Boulder, and his course, "Self and Consciousness," made a big difference for Amy and I, teaching us at a formative time to focus on creativity as a key element of personal expression and professional success.	I want to be like Jim, one of my professors at CU-Boulder years ago, because he continues to focus on personal growth and improving other people's lives later in his own life. He's clearly hitting the gas and avoiding cruise control.

Goals We Share, If Any	How I Will Follow and/or Stay Close to This Person
If I can make half as much difference for my clients, students, friends, and community as Jeff did for his, I'll be happy.	I think a lot about Jeff when I'm out running, and those of us who are mutual friends make a point to talk about him and honor his life.
Philippe and I both run consulting careers alongside our primary jobs, and we're both deeply committed to our families.	I'm lucky to be friends with Philippe, and I read about his groundbreaking work at rememberit.org.
Jay and I both coach athletes and enjoy helping them succeed in training, racing, and beyond.	I follow Jay's blog at coachjayjohnson.com, attend his seminars, and drop him an email every so often.
All three of us seek to make a difference and earn income in the athlete-entrepreneur space, and Robyn and Dean have paved the way for me.	I don't know Dean very well and I don't talk to Robyn often, but it's easy to follow their work at ultramarathonman.com and worldclassteams.com.
Amy and I share many goals, including traveling and adventuring, pursuing entrepreneurial endeavors that support our family and help other people, growing our relationship, and raising our kids.	Sometimes we assume that we'll be close to someone just because he or she is family. This isn't true. I'm lucky to work from home and spend a lot of time with my kids; Amy and I have been very intentional about setting up a life that allows us both to do plenty of parenting each day. I plan for one-on-one time with Amy, Wyatt, and Lila each day, and I'm pleased to report that I almost always succeed.
Jim is driven to generate meaningful change for his students and everyone else with whom he interacts, and I want to do the same. His presence is simultaneously grounding and inspiring—that's awesome and something for me to shoot for.	Jim's website, lifegardening.com, always provides a boost, and I refer to his book, *The Woo Way*, whenever I'm being pulled down by my own negative stories.

Person	Why I Want to Be Like Him or Her

Goals We Share, If Any	How I Will Follow and/or Stay Close to This Person

Mindset 2 ACTIVITY: Tour de "Wannabe" Bike Trainer Ride

Nothing helps a bike rider pass the time like pretending to be in the Tour de France! This workout is a great choice for those winter days when riding inside is the best option.

Mental training: It's always good to watch masters at their work— and to do so with the learning hat (or helmet) on.

Physical training: Boost your general riding fitness with time in the saddle, and increase power and speed with race-like efforts as described below.

When: Get fit early in the morning, late at night, or on cold winter days when riding outside is not possible.

How: Using an indoor bike trainer or stationary bike of some sort (a CompuTrainer is a great option because it provides power data, and I like using rollers that I can set my road bike on), complete a ride while watching a bike race on your TV or computer (or even phone or tablet). For this type of session, I like to find classic Tour de France stages online and mimic the race effort, sprinting when they sprint, climbing when they climb, and cruising when they cruise. Watching their tactics and riding techniques helps me learn and put the "wannabe" mindset into action. If you're looking for some exciting bike racing, consider going to www.youtube.com and searching "Tour de France climbs."

Extra: The "rollers"—imagine moving cylinders that your bike sits on top of, kind of like the infrastructure at the emissions testing facility—I mentioned are nice because they force you to pedal smoothly; if you don't, you'll tip right over! I learned to use my rollers by positioning myself in a doorway to build confidence; now I can stand up, sprint, and ride hard with a smooth cadence and pedal stroke.

Mindset 2 LEARN

Emma Roca

RACING LIFE

An international endurance-racing superstar, firefighter, and mother of three, Emma has long been recognized as Spain's Queen of the Extreme, and I faced her wrath many times as a competitor at international adventure races. One time, as we suffered up a steep, never-ending hike-a-bike under the hot Mexican sun, I turned to see Emma striding up the hill, passing our team with her bike on her back like we were standing still. Her three male teammates were nowhere to be seen, and Emma was soon out of site ahead of us. Awhile later, she ran past us going back down the hill, and then she passed us again going up the slope, this time carrying a male teammate's bike while the three of them struggled to keep up with her. She captained the winning team at the Adventure Racing World Championship in 2010, and, as you can see at her website (emmaroca.com), she's won a slew of adventure races, ultra runs, ski-mountaineering competitions, and other endurance events all over the world. Emma, 41, is now a top ultrarunner on the international scene, and I'm proud to call her my friend.

REAL LIFE

Emma is married to a great guy, David Rovira, and they have three young children. She stays busy with work as a mountain rescue firefighter (one of just a few women in Spain to do so), speaker, and author. She's working toward her doctorate in biochemistry, in part by conducting the SUMMIT Project to study ultradistance training and racing. We have been lucky to spend some family time with Emma, David, and their kids in Colorado and in Spain, and I'm always impressed by Emma's ability to intentionally apply lessons from racing in the other areas of her life. The resilience, positivity, and in-the-moment presence she has developed in racing have helped her in parenting, relationships, and work. Racing and work are clearly important to someone as driven as Emma, but it's also evident that family is her foundation and focus.

EMMA'S THOUGHTS ON BEING A WANNABE

Growing up as a female athlete in Spain in the '70s and '80s was challenging because I had few role models, and society dictated that I should probably be

(continues)

Mindset 2 LEARN (*continued*)

doing something else with my time. When I became one of the first five female professional firefighters in Catalonia in 1998, I faced further prejudice and more barriers. In many ways, most of my pursuits in racing and work have been an uphill battle as I have worked alongside female peers to pioneer a trail for other women.

When we decided to have children, though, I wanted to look for mothers who had been able to continue chasing their personal dreams while also dedicating themselves to family. Thankfully, I found a few of them, and learning from their examples has been important to my professional, family, and racing balance.

I look to Joane Somarriba, a cyclist who won the Tour de France, the Giro d'Italia, and the World Time Trial Championship, who is also a mother of three. Paula Radcliffe is an inspirational mom who also happens to hold the world record in the marathon. Josune Bereziartu is a world-class Basque rock climber who inspires me by rivaling the men in her sport.

Whether I am training for or racing in an ultra, fighting fires, doing medical research, or raising my own family, I find value in looking to others for positive examples.

—Emma

Find Your Carrot

"THIS EVENT IS NOT FOR THE MEEK OR INEXPERIENCED. It can be one of the most difficult winter events known."

It's right there in black and white on the application for the January 2004 Turquoise Lake 20-Miler, a high-altitude snowshoe race held in Leadville. The event, which started at an altitude of over 10,000 feet at the Sugar Loafin' Campground, ran for 20 consecutive years, and it was a favorite of ultrarunners, adventure racers, roadies, and anyone else up for suffering from Colorado and beyond.

Including me.

I'd driven that year from Boulder, where CU's spring semester was just starting, to Leadville specifically for this race. While it was my first time doing the 20-Miler, I was very familiar with running on snowshoes—which, in case you're not from a cold-weather climate, are not the tennis-racquet shoes you may have seen in old movies or paintings of Mountain Man types from the 1800s.

Modern snowshoes are comfortable and ultra-light, less than a pound in some cases. They're made of aluminum alloy and polyurethane-coated nylon and are much smaller than those high-strung clodhoppers of old. They look like little skateboards attached to your running shoes.

If you're a mountain athlete in Colorado, snowshoe running is just one of the things you do in winter. My dad did it, my dad's friends did it, and all the other runners and bikers and adventure racers I had come to know donned snowshoes in the winter. I had done my first snowshoe race at age 13 and hadn't stopped. Even in high school, I was competing. I'd have a varsity basketball game on Friday night, and the next morning my dad and I would drive up to Winter Park or Vail and do a 10K snowshoe race.

Doing the Turquoise Lake 20-Miler was taking it to another level. This was Olympic-level suffering—mixed with real danger, as the race waiver form reminds us. It makes for entertaining reading, provided you aren't just about to sign it:

WAIVER AND RELEASE: *I fully understand that participating in these snowshoe runs is very dangerous with hazards both apparent and hidden, and that I could easily become injured and/or die. . . . I acknowledge that I will be running in isolated, remote areas where aid and rescue may never arrive, and I agree to pay medical and rescue expenses I do incur. . . . I agree to have fun, try hard, and play fair!*

Yes, play fair, by all means! But make sure you don't get injured, as the medical aid station consists of a solitary jug of ice water sitting in the snow along the trail. If you do freeze to death, there are a couple of guys who patrol the course on snowmobiles, so don't worry—eventually you will be found.

The architect of this winter epic was Tom Sobal, the race director and a legendary mountain athlete. Sobal had won snowshoe races and trail races and was also a champion in a sport unique to the Colorado Rockies: burro racing—an activity rooted in the mining history of the region, where you run tethered to a pack animal. Burro racing, which I admit is one crazy sport I've never tried, is quite a spectacle. Ideally, the burro runs your pace. But some burros want to pick up the pace. So in these races, you see guys getting dragged along by their burros (which are crossbreeds between a horse and a donkey). Tom was never dragged, however. He had a legendary four-legged partner named Maynard, and the two were synched together in their running pace like lifelong training partners.

Sobal was a rare breed in another way, too, a throwback to the earliest days of the running boom when fields were small and almost everyone who ran was a serious competitor. He was a race director who actually ran—and won—his own races! When the field assembled at the start, he'd step forward and address us. "The lake ice this year is thin on top, so expect slush up to your knees," he would say. "And make sure you're carrying an extra jacket in case the wind picks up. Remember to take care of each other out there, and play fair!"

Then he'd walk back to the start, line up next to you, turn around, and say "Go!" Out of 20 editions of his race held from 1990 through 2009, Sobal won 15 of them.

The course included two crossings of Turquoise Lake, which at that time of year was like a layer cake of ice, with a firm coating on top and then over a foot of slush and then the solid lake ice. In some senses it was like running through a Carvel ice cream cake. For the first 3 miles, you were plowing knee-high slush. Let me tell you, there's nothing like getting out of a frigid Rocky Mountain lake in midwinter and then running 17 miles with soaked shoes encased in snow and ice.

During one particularly memorable 20-Miler, only 25 out of 64 starters finished, an astoundingly low percentage, particularly since the only people who start races like this are experienced mountain athletes. The race was held in blizzard conditions, and in the lead pack—of which I was part—we became disoriented as we crossed Turquoise Lake on the first part of the race. The course markers were covered in snow, however, so we didn't know where to go. Like a caravan of doomed polar explorers driven off course in the teeth of a ferocious storm, we drifted radically from the intended bearing. We finally reached the paved road that circumnavigates the lake and serves as part of the Leadville 100 run and bike courses in the summer. In the winter, it's a snowmobile and cross-country ski track. Sobal—who, as usual, was near the head of the pack—looked around and announced that we had come out at the wrong side of the lake. There was momentary hesitation among the leaders. What do we do? Scream? Protest? Denounce Sobal for organizing a race in these conditions, or ourselves for being foolish enough to participate? No, we huddled—and in a quick, democratic decision, it was agreed that we would simply run the course in reverse to make up the missing distance. Would it still be exactly 20 miles? No one knew, and I don't think anyone cared. Ultradistance events in extreme circumstances like this are not for people who stress about small details. We like to think of ourselves as "big-picture" types—insane, perhaps, but always trying to take a view that's as long as the road before us.

I think this perspective works in life, too. You work hard and create a detailed plan about what you're going to do. But all too often, things happen to derail these well-laid plans that are out of your control. You need to be nimble; you need to be ready to shift to changing circumstances, while keeping your eye on the ultimate goal.

A case in point was that Turquoise Lake 20-Miler when the blizzard blew through. The winner that day, on the improvised course, was yours truly (I actually beat Sobal himself, a rarity and an achievement). And I believe I was able to do it because I had quickly shifted my motivational source from the intrinsic ("I love snowshoe racing . . .

Snowshoeing is probably my favorite winter sport. It builds excellent cardiovascular fitness and strength without pounding the legs too much. CREDIT: JAN DePUY

Takes me back to my days as a kid . . . It's such a cool way to run in the winter . . . Turquoise Lake is so beautiful, and I feel so good being out here") to the extrinsic ("If I hang in there for the last 10 miles or so on this improvised course, I'll smoke the competition and will have had that rare privilege of beating Colorado's number-one snowshoeing legend himself!"). Don't get me wrong: those intrinsic motivations, which we'll discuss in more depth shortly, are a guiding force in life. But when things become less than enjoyable—which can happen routinely, not only in ultradistance racing, but in every aspect of life—dangling that "external" carrot in front of your face can really help you pull through.

There was another, related lesson we learned during that snowshoe race: the importance of being able to adjust quickly to changing conditions, especially when you're working or competing with others.

My dad saw this principle in action during his years competing in the Eco-Challenge. Every year, a team from an elite military organization—Navy SEALs, Rangers, Marines—would show up. The teams were composed of extraordinarily well-trained individuals; these competitors were super fit, superbly competent in all kinds of survival disciplines, and well integrated as teams.

So why did many of the military teams fail to finish?

Why didn't a Navy SEAL team win the Eco-Challenge every year?

Speaking to the *Chicago Tribune* about that very question in 1999, race founder and producer Mark Burnett said that while they certainly had the physical fitness, the military teams often lacked the necessary team skills to win. "After three days, everyone is down to zero energy, so everybody's equal at that point. That's when it becomes a test of character," he was quoted as saying. "In the first year, a 72-year-old great-grandmother finished, but a team of US Marines in their 20s didn't."

On SEAL-related forums and chat rooms at the time, several reasons for the SEALs' subpar performance were cited, including the fact that members of the US Navy's elite special force don't train specifically in the adventure disciplines like the mountain athletes do. I'm sure that's true.

But there's another reason, and in their candid moments, some of the military guys and gals admitted that this was one of the main factors, if not the main factor. In the military, everything is regimented. Even in the chaos of combat, you have a chain of command. In an adventure race, although no one is shooting at you, plans can go to hell just as quickly.

Adventure racing teams usually have a captain, but when the captain is too exhausted or sick or sleep-deprived to think straight (which happens to everyone over the course of one of these races), someone else has to step in to make decisions. Or maybe you get lost—and in adventure races you can get seriously lost, as in not knowing where the hell you are for five or ten hours. You might have to turn around and go right back up the mountain you just came down. One time in

Sweden, my teammate forgot his running shoes on a certain segment of the race and had to trek for more than 15 hours in his hard-soled mountain-biking shoes; it sucked, but there was no other option.

When stuff like that happens, decisions are made, challenges dealt with on the fly, kind of like what those of us in the lead pack did that morning during the Turquoise Lake snowshoe race. In an adventure race—where the scale of everything is magnified—if you've got everything planned down to the second and things go off script, and you're expecting through your training and experience that someone should assume a leadership role, *and* no one is sure just what the protocol is for that to happen in the unusual circumstances that you're in, your race crumbles.

That's part of what happened to the military teams.

Now please understand: I'm not disparaging Navy SEALs or any of our great Special Forces. I have friends and competitors who were Special Forces guys; as any American should, I salute them for their service, and I admire them tremendously. And, interestingly enough, I've found that as individuals, they do often demonstrate that improvisational ability. But as a team, at least as a team in adventure races like the Eco-Challenge, it didn't work out for them. Hey, nobody was fitter or tougher than those SEALs, yet a bunch of guys from Colorado—including a lawyer—finished ahead of them.

▲▲▲

I DID MY FIRST ADVENTURE RACE IN 2003. I HAD JUST FINISHED MY sophomore year at CU, and I knew my future as an athlete was not in track and field. So when my climbing buddy Mark Falender and I heard about a 24-hour event in Utah's Wasatch Mountains, we figured, "Let's do it."

Having a dad who'd done the Eco-Challenge, and having rubbed elbows and snowshoes with other athletes who had, I figured I was ready.

And I was wrong.

The first few hours of our race involved Mark and I paddling endlessly in circles as we tried to learn to steer our sit-on-top kayak (would have helped if we'd bothered to take it out at least once prior to the race). Not surprisingly, we were dead last by the time we reached the first checkpoint. But there was a lot of cycling involved in this race, Mark and I were both strong cyclists—and we were young. So we hammered for the rest of that first day, and then ran hard through the night. We ended up finishing second overall, out of about 50 teams—a respectable achievement for newbies.

The adrenaline rush of racing through the night, the technical challenges, the sense of working as part of a team to solve them, the logistics of making sure we had our nutrition . . . the whole thing just captivated me. I was hooked on adventure racing.

But now, another kind of adventure beckoned: I was pre-med at this point. I'd always liked the idea of helping people, and having seen what superbly skilled physicians were able to do to keep my mom alive—transplanting an organ—impressed and inspired me. I wanted to be able to do something like that to save a life, and to have that kind of direct effect on a person's survival. I also liked science, and I liked working hard. Heck, I was the valedictorian in my high school class at Evergreen, with a 4.0 average, so I felt I had the academic chops to handle it. Plus I was becoming more interested in anatomy and physiology from my budding endurance sports career.

Still, my dream and the careful plans I had crafted in my mind were about to change. After wrestling one too many nights with organic chemistry, I'd had enough. I came to the conclusion that I needed to change my life by spending less time with books and more time with girls. I was lonely, and I needed to meet someone. I made that decision, and two days later, I went to a play in Denver with a student group. On that trip, I met a smart, spunky senior named Amy. We started dating, and life got a lot better, immediately. I'm really glad I had the wisdom to realize I needed a change. Ten years later, Amy and I are the happily married parents of two children.

I got my first big opportunity as an adventure racer that fall, when I was invited to race Adventure Xstream Expedition Moab. Adam Chase had organized a team sponsored by Eastern Mountain Sports, a major national outdoor equipment retail chain, and Salomon, one of the world's largest manufacturers of sporting goods. Adam, who lives in Boulder, is a runner and adventure racer who knew my dad, and we had met at one of the snowshoe races the previous winter. Along with two very impressive sponsors, he'd assembled quite a team for the race. But he was one person shy, and decided to take a chance on an inexperienced kid. There was money and prestige on the line for him. And this wasn't just a question of picking me as a teammate in a relay race, where he might hand me a baton for my leg and barely see me before and after. In adventure racing, you're together for days—and nights—on end, working cheek to jowl, in very difficult circumstances and challenging conditions. Adam was taking a risk, and making a commitment to me, a college kid. I still appreciate that.

That said, I will admit that there was a momentary hesitation when I thought about my friends at CU, who would no doubt be staying up late the week I was racing, to party and chase girls. But Amy and I were getting serious at that point and she supported my racing. So even at age 21, I was beginning to get a sense of what my future was shaping up to be; and while it would no longer include organic chemistry, it probably wasn't going to involve a great deal of time clubbing, either. Don't get me wrong: I liked going out and socializing until dawn as much as the next 21-year-old. But I knew that if I was going to be a serious athlete, which seemed to be the goal emerging after I shifted course from med school, I couldn't do both. Training starts early. Partying goes on late. Hence, my life as a party animal ended almost as quickly as it began.

Moab is a great place for mountain biking and other adventure sports. In this shot, I'm trying to keep control during 24 Hours of Moab, a mountain biking race in which athletes ride as many loops as they can on a technical trail over a nonstop day and night. CREDIT: MOAB ACTION SHOTS

Part of the allure here was Moab, "an off road Nirvana," as one blogger puts it; a place that's become almost synonymous with "X-treme" (or however you choose to spell it) sports. Moab has vast canyons, dramatically fluctuating temperatures, the Colorado River, the Slickrock Bike Trail, plus (at least when it rains) tons of what Dad calls "Moab Mud," a particularly difficult variety of saturated soil to slog through that is formed from the sandstone that predominates here.

The Xstream Expedition would involve almost four days of nonstop racing in this "desert wonderland" with the typical adventure-racing disciplines of trekking, mountain biking, kayaking, and fixed ropes. Teams of four would cover many of the famous desert trails, canyons, and rivers around Moab, and we'd also traverse the high La Sal Mountains east of town. The October timing of the event meant we could face extremely hot days in the desert and cold (and possibly snowy) nights in the mountains.

Adam, then 40, was the captain, but his full-time job was as a tax lawyer. He also wrote articles for some of the trail and off-road running magazines. Adam was an experienced and enthusiastic adventure racer and a sharp, entrepreneurial guy. With the exception of one 21-year-old rookie from Colorado, he had surrounded himself with some experienced, tough adventure racers.

Andrew Hamilton was a speed climber who had summited all 54 of Colorado's peaks of 14,000 feet and over, one after another, in some insanely fast time. He had been leading the team all season on mountain biking sections, and if that wasn't enough, this impressively well-rounded athlete was also our best paddler.

Emily Baer was easily the strongest runner on our team. She was the youngest finisher in history to complete the Hardrock 100, a triple-digit run considered even more difficult than Leadville, because it's at higher altitude and has more climbs. She was 23 when she finished Hardrock—very young for a top ultra-endurance athlete (many of the top ultramarathoners don't hit their peak until their late thirties or even their forties). She lived in the remote mountains in a custom-built home with her husband, Ernst, who would be Dad's crewing buddy for the race.

Yes, once again, my father was going to be part of my adventure. Having an Eco-Challenge veteran like Mark Macy around was a good idea. He might even help keep his newbie son on his toes.

And then there was me, 21-year-old now-formerly-pre-med-student Travis, who could identify most of the major organs on a human anatomy chart, but certainly hadn't proven that he had the heart of a champion adventure racer. I was, however, the son of "Mace" Macy, whom everyone knew, and who would be there as part of the crew, just in case anyone wanted to make comparisons ("You're okay as an adventure racer, Travis, but you're no Mace Macy").

Yes, there was a little pressure on me! Plus, the Expedition served as the series finale for Adventure Xstream, the main adventure-racing series in the western states, and while our team was one of the favorites, we had serious competition from Team Crested Butte. They were sponsored by Crested Butte Mountain Resort, but the members of the team all lived in Gunnison, Colorado, an Old West cow-town on the western slope that teems with world-class athletes. In Gunnison, just about everyone has a nickname (including the town itself, known as "Gunni"), and our rivals were local legends.

There was Jon Brown, known to all as "JB," an articulate, tan, pro mountain biker who could also run with the best of them; and Eric "Sully" Sullivan, a Kansas farm boy who looked like a So Cal surfer. Good-looking, muscular, tan, and with a head of long, curly blond hair, Sully had come to Gunni as a student at Western State Colorado University and stayed for the mountain biking and skiing. He's an amazing athlete.

The Crested Butte team also included Bryan "Wick" Wickenhauser, one of these Daniel Boone–type adventure racers who could seemingly do anything. I observed Wick a lot during that first race, and it was he who made me realize that there was such a thing as an Ultra Mindset. I'd already been around plenty of folks before who exemplified it, from my dad to Mike Kloser to Tom Sobal, but it was Wick's demeanor and performance in this race that made it all click, when I told myself: *To do this kind of stuff well, you have to be thinking differently.*

Wick was always thinking: because it involves flexibility and flying by the seat of your pants, the Ultra Mindset is inherently a creative and efficient mindset, and Wick demonstrated these qualities in every aspect of his life. He's the kind of guy who uses energy bar wrappers to reinforce the punctured sidewalls of flat mountain-bike tires on the racecourse, and who combines training time and kids' naptime at home by pulling the little ones in a sled while he cross-country skis.

One of the cool things about adventure racing is that every team must have members of both sexes. We had Emily, and Crested Butte had Jari Kirkland, an icon in western racing and a terror for me.

Jari smoked me at the 24 Hours of Moab mountain-bike race, twice. The thought of turning around during the race and seeing her on a mountain bike, closing fast, haunted me throughout the race. "That's all I need!" I said to myself. "To get smoked by the female of the competitors' team." No one would care that it was a superwoman who beat me. I imagined the Gunni cowboys celebrating wildly, probably firing six-shooters while riding around bareback on burros, for all I knew. I imagined my teammates standing by in shocked, dejected silence, and also saw the image of my dad standing by the support truck, shaking his head with disappointment.

I had to find this Ultra Mindset, and I had to find it now!

The truth is, it would come gradually, slowly, day by day, race by race, year by year. But as I fretted over the Crested Butte team, I never imagined that someday they would be both my teammates and my guides to the secrets of that Ultra Mindset.

Of course, none of that would have happened if I had screwed the pooch in Moab.

In addition to bragging rights in the western world of adventure sports, the winning team would earn about $8,000 in prize money, which worked out to $2,000 per person. That's good dough for a regional adventure race. For a 21-year-old newbie to the sport, who made $9 an hour tutoring football players at CU, it represented a potentially Lotto-like payday. When I heard what I could be making, I was suddenly psyched, energized, and rarin' to go. Bring on the competition! I was ready to kick Butte.

Adventure races have a traditional start, with teams lined up and a gun firing, but the real race begins the day before, when race officials distribute the previously undisclosed maps and course details to the teams. Everybody immediately crowds around the map to see what

Safety under pressure is very important when it comes to fixed ropes in adventure racing. That's especially true with big, overhanging rappels like this 175-foot drop near Moab's Gemini Bridges. CREDIT: WWW.AXSRACING.COM / WWW.NEWCOMERPHOTO.COM

the event holds in store. While running races, triathlons, and most other endurance events follow an established course and distance, adventure races follow the land and geographic features. Where there's a river, paddle; if there's a mountain on the route, climb it; when you come to a rock wall, rappel down it. There's no going around these obstacles. In adventure racing, you meet the environment head on. Although you may know ahead of time which disciplines will be involved, you don't know the exact course, distances, or order until they're revealed just before race. When the maps are finally distributed, a crazy scramble ensues, with navigators frantically trying to add checkpoints from grid coordinates to determine the best routes to get there, while other team members are running around moving shoes, climbing gear, bikes, packs, paddles, food, water, personal flotation devices, clothing, climbing gear, emergency supplies, and other items to various piles and bins all over the hotel room or campsite, so that the support crew will have them waiting at the correct checkpoint (you don't want your climbing gear waiting for you on the banks of the river you're supposed to paddle across).

Our Moab race followed this pattern, and we were relieved to finally get on the course itself, along with 45 other teams, when the gun went off at 12:01 a.m. (yes, this race started one minute after midnight . . . just to keep people on their toes).

Getting up to the La Sal Mountains from Moab requires climbing almost 4,000 vertical feet on steep roads and narrow, single-track trails, but the hard work was more than worth it when we came upon the golden aspen forests that would provide an autumn-in-the-desert background for a whole day and night of trekking from checkpoint to checkpoint. Team Crested Butte was in constant pursuit as we navigated through the mountains; we were too rushed to stop for photos, but pleased to enjoy vast canyon-land panoramas around every corner. The La Sals are an island of peaks surrounded by desert, and when you get up high, the view of deep valleys, tall spires, and vertical walls is never ending.

Despite the majestic scenery, my teammates were anxious, none of them more so than I. We knew from experience that disaster could be around any corner, and we were committed to working together and keeping our heads in the game to avoid just that.

In a long adventure race, you are finally settled in to some sort of a rhythm by the second day. Ours included meeting briefly with Dad and Ernst every six hours or so at a checkpoint, where they loaded us up with food, water, and fresh gear. That is, if they decided to stick around for the meeting. Unlike some crew members who try to fix every little issue experienced by their racers, Dad is never one for "babying" me (or anyone else, for that matter) when crewing. Ernst was the same way. They're not bellhops, is how they saw it; they're not shrinks;

and they're not personal assistants. They're there to take the stuff from point A to point B. Period. They'd often left our gear at the checkpoint and then headed off for a hike or run of their own.

Had I been expecting a foot massage from my dad at the checkpoint, I would have been disappointed.

Still, even though he wasn't indulging my every whim, having Dad at my first big, professional adventure race helped me, particularly the last two nights of the four-day race.

By then we had left the Gold Bar Campground west of Moab on the Colorado River, and were now grunting on bikes up the endless and aptly named Long Canyon, which climbs 2,156 feet over 7.57 steep, rocky miles to a plateau above. The sun had set long ago, and though we knew Crested Butte was not far behind, the only sounds in the darkness were the faint echoes of our breathing and our shifting gears reverberating off the canyon walls.

As I rotated my feet in laborious circles on the pedals, grinding down my spirit as I ground out yard after painful yard of trail, I remember thinking that what I'd really like to do is stop, put down my bike, and go to sleep. Enough with this stupid race. Maybe organic chemistry wasn't so bad after all. But then I flashed back to Dad in his first 100-mile race at Leadville. He might not have been ready; he probably wanted to stop many times. But he didn't. He finished. And one of the main reasons was that he was thinking about the reward at the end: seeing his family.

I needed to focus on my reward, too. It may sound crass to admit it, but a dollar sign immediately formed in my head. Two thousand smackeroos. So what if it wasn't as warm and fuzzy as Dad's goal?

I kept going.

Mine wasn't the only patience frazzled at that point. As any parent knows, the second night without sleep is when you begin to run out of self-control. And if you have been riding up a steep, rocky trail in

Long Canyon is a long, tough grind up a rocky jeep trail. We were somewhere near this point in the middle of the night when Andrew made his compelling, pro-fane, and (in hindsight) humorous call to action. CREDIT: WWW.AXSRACING.COM / WWW.NEWCOMERPHOTO.COM

Moab for a few hours, that self-control muscle is about to tear like a ruptured Achilles' tendon.

As we headed up the canyon, Adam recommended to the three of us that we stop to nap for 10 minutes. Such catnaps are fairly common in these situations, and a quick rest can really rejuvenate the body and mind. The idea pulled me out of my stupor, and I was about to utter some form of agreement before happily curling up in the trail for a proper nap, when Andrew's shout rattled me to the core.

"Adam, we're not all rich fucking lawyers!"

We were thunderstruck. Talk about loss of self-control, especially for a guy who had been mild-mannered, polite, and quiet for the entire race to that point.

While Andrew's language may have been inappropriate, he was correct about where our thinking needed to be at the moment. What he was really saying was, "Maybe you don't need the money, Adam, but we do. And the only way we're going to get it is to keep pushing, because the competition is right on our tail, and they will take our money away from us if they pass us."

Had there been a psychologist riding shotgun with us, he might have put it a different way: we needed to shift our focus to an extrinsic motivation. The personal attack—and I'm glad to report that Andrew and Adam were both laughing about it just a few hours later—was actually Andrew's rallying cry for the team. He was calling on a powerful extrinsic motivator, in this case, the money we could win by finishing first. Indeed, Andrew was *not* a rich lawyer, and his pregnant wife was gathering debt in medical school.

His call to action provided a better pickup than a quick nap on the trail, and we soon found ourselves rolling along, strategizing, and working as a team once again. By shifting toward the external motivator, we had provided relief to the waning self-control sector of the brain. Now we were hungry again.

The race continued. After a descent on our mountain bikes of around 2,000 feet near Gemini Bridges, we hit a checkpoint, and then we turned to *go right back up* on our bikes. "Who planned this sadistic route?" I remember thinking to myself. After going down, up, and back down on our bikes, we then had to run along a section of the storied 142-mile Kokopelli Trail, and then paddle for hours on the Colorado River. All this time, the members of Team Crested Butte—who must have been properly motivated themselves—were right on our heels, and often in sight just behind us. But throughout, we kept reminding ourselves of the prize, articulating it to each other, which I think made the motivation almost tangible.

Andrew talked about how important the money would be for his wife's mounting medical-school bills (hearing about the size of these bills, I was certain that changing my major had been a good idea). Emily considered the value of $2,000 for the remote lifestyle she shared with Ernst in the mountains. Even the "rich" lawyer, Adam, would benefit. After all, he wasn't a hedge-fund manager. He had kids, and those kids had expenses, and would eventually be going to college. A little extra cash would help him, too (as I knew, being the son of a lawyer who had taken years to get his practice rolling).

As for me, it was just assumed that the 21-year-old needed money. What 21-year-old doesn't? But my financial needs were different: after much prompting by my teammates, I admitted that I might use it to buy a new bike and also take Amy out to her favorite Thai restaurant in Boulder for some of those Pad Thai noodles she loved.

"Awww, that's so cute," Emily said, as I blushed under my sunburn.

Keeping these external "carrots" in mind kept us going hard as we dealt with sleep deprivation, desert heat, and deep fatigue over the final 24 hours (that's the homestretch in an adventure race). A photo finish for LeMond and Hinault in the Tour de France meant a literal sprint to the line, but in a long adventure race, a team is "breathing down your neck" anytime they're within an hour or so. In Moab, Team Crested Butte was just a few minutes behind us going into the final paddling segment, a three-hour kayak down the Colorado River through a deep and gorgeous sandstone canyon. That moment on the bike climb could have been the point where we blew it, and where the more experienced team came from behind to take the victory. But our carrots were ripe and large and inviting in our minds that day. We knew that our only route to victory, even at this late stage of the race, was to stay focused on what we were racing for, and keep the hammer down until the finish line just east of Moab.

Paddling hard to the finish, we won the race! We fist-bumped and high-fived each other. "I'm proud of you, Bud," said my dad as he put his arm around me. Even the taciturn mountain man, Ernst, gave me a hug. Our team captain, Adam, the lawyer, took me aside. "I may not have as much money as Andrew thinks I have, but I'm pretty smart," he said with a smile. "I selected you for the team, didn't I?"

Victory always feels good, but winning for the first time in a new sport, in front of my dad, and knowing that I'd held my weight among a group of national-class competitors really made it truly memorable. So did the $2,000 check. Although, here's the last point about that: a decade later, I can't remember exactly how I spent the money. Some of it may even still be sitting around in my bank account. But the feelings I had that day, with my teammates and my dad, will always be with me.

In other words, the extrinsic motivation got me across the finish line; but the intrinsic rewards are the ones that will last a lifetime.

Ultra Mindset 3: Find Your Carrot

MOTIVATION IS WHAT GETS PEOPLE UP OFF THEIR BUTTS. MOTIVATION is what gets things done. No motivation means no pyramids, no great works of art, no corporate empires, no great athletic feats.

"Motivation produces," declared Edward L. Deci and Richard M. Ryan, the acknowledged authorities on the topic.

But, as the two prominent psychologists have explained in their many influential articles and books, including "Intrinsic and Extrinsic Motivations: Classic Definitions and New Directions," published in the journal *Contemporary Educational Psychology*, there are different kinds of motivation. The most basic distinction is between *intrinsic motivation*, which they define as "doing something because it is inherently interesting or enjoyable," and *extrinsic motivation*, which refers to doing something "because it leads to a separable outcome."

We all know which of these two types of motivation is considered pure, noble, and true: Right, the motivation that comes from within. Extrinsic motivation, by comparison, is dismissed as superficial, or somehow selfish or bad. "Extrinsic motivation has typically been characterized as a pale and impoverished form of motivation," noted Deci and Ryan, who are both on the faculty at the University of Rochester in New York.

They have argued that not only is extrinsic motivation powerful, but it may be even more effective for some people, and in some situations, than intrinsic motivation. Here's an example, also from "Intrinsic and Extrinsic Motivations":

> A student who does his homework only because he fears parental sanctions for not doing it is extrinsically motivated because he is doing the work in order to attain the separable outcome of avoiding sanctions. Similarly, a student who does the work because she personally believes it is valuable for her chosen career is also extrinsically motivated because she too is doing it for its instrumental value rather than because she finds it interesting.

I'm no research psychologist, but as an educator, a professional endurance athlete, and a coach, I think I know a thing or two about motivation in action; and I can speak to the truth of Deci and Ryan's observations. I'd add that while perhaps less noble and pure in some people's minds, extrinsic motivations are often pragmatic and practical.

Speaking as a former high-school English teacher, I have to admit that, sure, I'd love to have students read Shakespeare because they are genuinely fascinated by the Bard's use of language, or the great characters he created and the intricate plots he constructed. But I know that students with that kind of motivation are rare. I'm okay if they read *Macbeth* or *Hamlet* because they know some questions about it are going to appear on the final; even better, if they dream of going to law school someday and figure that a passing familiarity with the greatest writer in history will mark them as an educated person and give them a leg up.

Deci and Ryan say it can almost turn into a looping mechanism: extrinsic rewards lead to a feeling of competence, and that, in turn, enhances the intrinsic motivation. A compliment from the boss, a positive online review of your work, recognition by your colleagues, a bonus or promotion—all are separable (extrinsic) outcomes that loop back to a feeling of competence and increased intrinsic motivation.

Of course, other factors outside of performance also dictate your next bonus or performance, and if your boss is an ungrateful, ungenerous ass, you may never get the compliment you think you deserve.

This is another reason, in my opinion, why running and other endurance sports have become so popular. Put aside the health benefits for a minute, and consider: Where else in life do you create and take such direct control over your own extrinsic rewards? Where else in life are the outcomes directly determined by what you as an individual do—not you and a spouse (as in parenting), you as part of a corporate or organizational structure (as in your work life), but you? Where else can you do all that, and still have fun?

Mindset 3 REFLECTION

As a coach, I see the way recreational endurance athletes motivate themselves. They want to do their first ultramarathon, at least in part, so that they can post it on Facebook; so that they can earn bragging rights among their training group; so that they can impress their boyfriend or girlfriend. Chances are that along the training journey, they will find deeper reasons. But if what's motivating them to do the 20-milers I have scheduled for them this Sunday is simply the thought of 75 "Likes" on their finish-line photo on Facebook . . . fine!

And if I told you that the *only* reason I continue racing is for the inner joy it gives me . . . baloney. I'm not a rich lawyer, either, so the prize money I can earn is certainly part of what gets me up in the morning and out onto the trails.

Finding your carrot, regardless of whether it turns out to be a zucchini, or, heck, even a popsicle, is an important component of the Ultra Mindset. Let's find yours:

List three meaningful and challenging pursuits in your life:

1) _____

_____

_____

_____

2) _____

_____

_____

_____

3) _____

_____

_____

_____

Then answer these questions for each of the three:

I am motivated intrinsically because

_____

_____

_____

_____

_____

But I can tell this intrinsic motivation is tiring when

_____

_____

_____

_____

When that happens, I could utilize extrinsic motivators by telling myself

_____

_____

_____

_____

_____

Now utilize these motivators during your next workout—or challenge in life!

Here's how I answered them, by the way:

Macy's Motivations

Three meaningful and challenging pursuits in my life are

Parenting

In the first pursuit, I am motivated intrinsically because:
I love my kids and have worked hard to develop a flexible work schedule that gives me many long, full days with my one- and three-year-old.

But I can tell this intrinsic motivation is tiring when:
By midafternoon, the house is a total mess, both kids are crying, and I kind of feel like doing the same.

At this time, I could utilize extrinsic motivators by:
Telling myself that taking care of my kids not only saves us daycare money, but could eventually result in less hassle for me when they are teenagers because of our solid foundation together, and even increased income for them as adults because of the social and educational contributions and impact I can provide.

Endurance Racing

In the second pursuit, I am motivated intrinsically because:
I love to be outside, and training hard makes me feel good physically and mentally.

But I can tell this intrinsic motivation is tiring when:
It's time to get up early for another run or to do another session on the treadmill while the baby is napping or my legs are trashed from a long race.

At this time, I could utilize extrinsic motivators by:
Telling myself that persevering in this is a way to earn money and positive recognition for my consulting work.

High-Performance Consulting

In the third pursuit, I am motivated intrinsically because:
I thoroughly enjoy helping athletes, companies, audiences, and readers as they work to achieve their goals.

But I can tell this intrinsic motivation is tiring when:
It's midnight, I'm tired, the one-year-old is up, and one of my athletes has just sent me a long email about a problem he or she is having with training, or a race that didn't go as planned.

At this time, I could utilize extrinsic motivators by:
Telling myself that persistence and continued hard work will pay off in income and increased business, leading to more opportunities for my family and less stress about things like paying for college.

Mindset 3 ACTIVITY: Best Bang for Your Buck: High-Altitude Snowshoe

Snowshoeing is a fun and unique activity. And, if there's no snow around, completing this workout with a traditional hike is an excellent alternative.

Mental training: Snowshoeing high in the mountains is always challenging, and it can also be cold and miserable. It's often a whole lot of fun, too!

Physical training: Build leg strength, aerobic fitness, and high-altitude specificity by running and/or hiking on snowshoes somewhere between 9,000 and 12,000 feet. Snowshoeing at altitude provides a big bang for the buck because of the intense leg strength work and serious lung burn.

When: I try to snowshoe at least once a week in the winter; doing it even once or twice can be fun and beneficial.

How: Use regular running shoes with lightweight snowshoes made for running. (See snowshoeracing.com or visit my website, travismacy.com, where I post free training videos on snowshoeing, and check out my training videos on snowshoes.) The running snowshoes are light and fast, nothing like the old tennis rackets you're imagining! They're 8 by 20 inches and weigh 32 ounces per pair. Drive to a trailhead, or make it a weekend trip, and get out there! Be sure to bring adequate clothing, food, water, and safety gear (waterproof jacket, emergency blanket, and avalanche beacon, shovel, and probe if you're headed into some serious backcountry). And don't forget your camera for the views!

Warm Weather Alternate

If you're not in a place where there's snow, go for a hike on a hilly trail. Or head down to the beach and jog or walk in the soft sand. Or if you can't stand the heat, you could even just get on the stair-climber in the gym.

While you're doing it, think about what's motivating you—intrinsically or extrinsically. At the start, think intrinsic: the enjoyable mental break you are getting from your busy workday; the natural high you're feeling from endorphins. As you get tired, go extrinsic. All the things we said before—social media boasting, moderate food or drink rewards—all apply, in order to help keep you motivated.

Mindset 3 LEARN

Dave Mackey

RACING LIFE

Dave was named *UltraRunning Magazine*'s 2011 North American Ultra Runner of the Year and has won numerous events, from 50K to multiday races. He is still setting course records even at age 44, including at the 31-year-old Quad Dipsea in Marin, California (see davemackey .blogspot.com). Dave and I adventure-raced together with Team Spyder, and we remember fondly the times we've spent dragging each other along through deserts, mountains, and more.

REAL LIFE

Dave is a committed father of two young kids and a dedicated husband. I am inspired by his drive to start and complete a dual degree, a master's in physician assistant studies along with a master's in public health, in his early forties. He now practices medicine in Boulder, Colorado, while running professionally and spending plenty of time with his family. He's a nice, down-to-earth guy, and I'm sure you'd enjoy having a cup of coffee with him on Boulder's Pearl Street after a long run.

DAVE'S THOUGHTS ON FINDING YOUR CARROT

When I decided to go back to school to become a physician's assistant at age 39, I knew I had my work cut out for me. I took classes at nights and on weekends. My wife, a teacher, stepped up bigtime, taking on more of the responsibility as breadwinner during the time I had to cut back on my work hours. PA school was perhaps the hardest thing I've ever done. And yet, at the same time, I won North American Ultra Runner of the year.

How did I do it? Well, in part, I showed up. Showed up for my runs, showed up for my classes, showed up when it was time to hit the books. I stayed up late studying, got up early to run, and trained while listening to recorded audio lectures from my classes. I did what I had to do to reach my goal. In the process, I learned that perceived limits are the product of experience. I learned also how important it is to quit whining, buck up, and keep plugging. My old high-school cross-country coach used to say that 90 percent of the time, when you think you can't go any faster, you probably can. I think that's true about life, work, career. You probably can do more than you thought. You just need to find that carrot.

—Dave

Have an Ego and Use It—
Until It's Time to Put
Your Ego Aside

"TRAV. TRAV, GET UP. TRAV!"

The distant, Aussie accent sounded vaguely familiar, but when I opened my eyes, read 4:21 a.m. on my
watch, saw a cloudy but sun-brightened sky, touched
a helmet on my head that had probably been used as
a pillow, brushed a coat of snow off my sleeping bag,
and felt the cold pavement on which I had been slum-
bering so deeply, I knew I was in a strange place.

Momentary panic shifted to overwhelming confu-
sion. Why was it light out this early? How come my
head hurt so bad? Why were my feet throbbing? How
did my mouth get so raw, and why were my lips covered with sores? Did I really have blisters on my ass? It

sure felt like I did. Why was I starting to shiver uncontrollably? Was I really *this* hungry? Unbelievable.

"Trav! Get the hell up!"

Darren's harsh but matter-of-fact tone snapped me back to reality.

The hustled gear scramble of my teammates, Darren Clarke, Paul Romero, and Karen Lundgren, reminded me that we had been sleeping in the parking lot of a truckers' outpost in a remote area of northern Sweden that served as a checkpoint for the Explore Sweden Adventure Race. This was day three of the race, and my journey had already taken me to dark, cold places that made Moab, the previous year, seem like a pleasant stroll in the sun. Explore Sweden 2005 was my first international expedition race, and I was a still-green 22-year-old on a team of gritty, experienced athletes who were racing for the podium against the best teams from Sweden, France, New Zealand, Australia, the United States, Norway, Russia, Poland, and elsewhere. It was one thing to beat the team from Crested Butte—you take on a menagerie of Aussies or Kiwis in an adventure race, and you might as well be shooting hoops against a team of Lebron Jameses and Kevin Durants.

We needed our "A" game. And right now it was a "B–" at best. During the first paddling section, our two-person sea kayak flipped over in a large, fast-moving, ice-lined river. After a dreadful swim in cold whitewater, we somehow righted it and continued forward. The long, narrow lake at the end of the river was covered with thin ice. As we forged on, kayaks in tow, to the transition area at the end of the lake, we repeatedly broke through the ice and had to use picks to pull ourselves out of the water. The ice picks have small, wooden handles and a nail coming out the end, connected to each other with a string that runs through your jacket like children's mittens. They were part of the head-spinning list of mandatory gear for this race, along with the personal flotation devices and wetsuits that kept us from sinking into the cold Swedish waters. Still, it was cold. Very cold, especially under the ice. After a mile or so of that, we reached a transition area. There we stripped naked in the snowy air, donned cycling clothes, and built up our bikes from the pieces that had been packed into boxes for transportation to the remote location; and then we rode out into the swamp, where, hours later, using a technique not likely to be recommended by your local bike shop, we would have to urinate on our frozen cycles to make the frozen chains spin again.

That was the first half of the first day.

We later navigated on foot through an endless orienteering section in a swamp with thin ice (fragile enough to break through, solid enough to cut the shins) just above cold, knee-deep water. The race also involved portage: that's when you carry your kayaks or roll them on carts from one body of water to the next. Those suckers are heavy— and we had one portage that spanned almost 20 miles of pavement.

Kayak paddling is one of the three most important adventure-racing disciplines, in addition to trekking and mountain biking. Although I was a pretty good paddler by the time this photo was taken in Abu Dhabi in 2009, I had almost no paddling experience in Explore Sweden 2005—and I suffered immensely because of it. CREDIT: WOUTER KINGMA

Nights involved extended daylight at the high latitude with an hour or so of sleep on the side of the trail before we woke up shivering and disoriented.

The race had been brutally cold, with plenty of snow and rain, and some of the top teams had dropped out on account of illness, injury, and for the simple fact that a lot of this was not very fun. Among those who had to call it quits was Mike Kloser's Team Nike ACG / Balance Bar, hands-down the best team in the world.

In short, the Explore Sweden race was forcing me to explore heretofore undiscovered levels of suffering—levels that had stopped the planet's top adventure-racing team and one of the toughest guys I know dead in their tracks.

I was exhausted, sleep-deprived, and completely wrecked from head to toe when I stumbled into the small shack next to that truck stop and made the mistake of looking in a mirror. My eyes were bloodshot, my hair was matted, my face was puffy and red. Blisters lined my lips. I felt even worse than I looked, and I was pretty sure that I wasn't going to last much longer racing through the frozen north. I began to think that Darren, Paul, and Karen had made a mistake inviting me to join their team. They'd been impressed with my credentials, and what I had done in helping Team EMS / Salomon win in Moab, and so they took a chance. But I was over my head—and out of my mind.

Looking at myself in the mirror, I began contemplating a peaceful end to the race then and there. I began fantasizing about the comforts of a warm hotel that could be mine within an hour if I just threw up my hands and said "no mas." I realized this was the moment of truth. Would I listen to my body, brain, and feelings, which all sent a resounding message that quitting the race was clearly the path to take, or would I pursue the dream of finishing my first multiday, nonstop adventure race on the international scene?

I'm eternally grateful that, when looking in the mirror at the zombie-like face staring back at me, I remembered my dad again at his first Leadville, and the Ultra Mindset attitude he had impressed upon his son. I remembered Sobal and LeMond and Ulrich and all the other tough guys I'd looked up to over the years who had been in the very same place I was then at one time or another. They didn't opt for the Hilton, and neither should I. And, of course, there were my current teammates. The four of us had stood together, united on the starting line days ago, and pledged not to quit. So now I would be going back on my word if I threw in the towel.

I remembered, most important and most of all, my ego.

Yes, the ego. My ego said I could, should, and must do it. And I did it.

By ego, I'm not talking about the Freudian concept in which the ego is the rational component of personality that helps to mediate between the id and the real world. The way I'm using ego here (and the common usage) is ego as in "egotism": conceit, self-importance. Or in self-esteem or self-image.

All of mine had tanked that morning in Sweden. Esteem, image, self-importance, confidence. I needed to reach back to that "conceit" part of the ego—the part that can be shamed or embarrassed as I would have been had I dropped out. Kloser might be able to get away with it, but I didn't have his credentials. Still, I reminded myself that I had already won some major ultradistance events of various kinds; that I had been part of a winning team in Moab, my first time out of the gate in adventure racing, beating one of the toughest teams in North America in the process (the Gunni guys and gals). I reminded myself that I was Mace Macy's son; that in a sense I'd been bred to do this. Mountain biking in the Rockies at age 5. Snowshoeing in winter since junior high. Running at altitude year round. It wasn't your typical American childhood, and I knew it. I had been raised and trained to be an outdoor endurance athlete. And now I was ready to chuck it all away so that I could have clean sheets for one night? There'd be plenty of warm rooms and comforts when this race was over. It was time to step up.

Thus spoke my ego.

I walked out of that remote outpost with a smile on my face and a fire in my heart, and we hopped—well, slowly climbed—onto our bikes with skis and snowshoes duct-taped to them, then pedaled down the road.

Forty miles of mountain biking brought us to a transition area where we dismantled our bikes for the fourth or fifth time in the race, packed them in bike boxes, and loaded them on a semitruck that would transport them to the finish.

We continued forward on the race's signature stage, a challenging, 36-hour segment involving a mix of trekking, skiing, snowshoeing, winter mountaineering, and via ferrata (big in Europe, this skill essentially involves rock climbing in a place where metal holds and cables have been drilled into the rock for protection; you use protective slings and carabiners but no ropes). We carried gear for all of these disciplines and chose between trekking, snowshoeing, and skiing based on the conditions.

And those conditions were about to get worse: in the middle of the night, as we were slogging through a cross-country skiing segment of the winter alpine stage, a blizzard blew up. It happened just as we all were starting to fall asleep on our skis, leaning on the poles for support. Karen's feet needed some attention, but we knew that stopping in the blizzard could be life-threatening.

Skiing about 30 yards ahead of the group—any further would have meant I was out of sight and possibly out of teammates—I spotted a small, wooden shack. It couldn't have been any larger than 10 by 10 feet, and its walls, no taller than my head, were covered almost entirely in snowdrifts. Nonetheless, it looked secure—and anything was better than the howling wilderness we appeared to be wandering around in.

"Guys!" I shouted, "I think there's a building!"

Paul's response, driven by both his care for Karen and his desire to finish the race by making it through the night, was immediate: "We're going in."

Darren used his ice ax and snowshoes to begin digging out the 4 feet of snow that covered half the door.

We soon found ourselves inside of the Adventure Racing Holy Grail: a dry dwelling with a woodstove, wood, and newspaper. The fire was blazing within minutes, and I didn't even wake up when I fell off the little bench I was sleeping on.

Possibly because it occurred in a warm room instead of a frozen parking lot, this hour of rest proved more rejuvenating than the last. Constant wetness often makes the feet of ultrarunners and adventure racers swollen and tender (imagine your feet after hours in a bathtub), and the fire provided the first dry-out in days. Karen reapplied duct tape on the particularly blistered areas on her heels before giving us, in her typically positive and matter-of-fact tone, the go signal: "Okay, let's do this."

We headed out into what had thankfully become a sunny early morning ready to take on the world, or at least this rather unforgiving

Ego and teammates got me through some cold, snowy conditions out there in Sweden. We carried skis, snowshoes, crampons, climbing gear, and winter clothing for this long section toward the end of the race. CREDIT: TRAVIS MACY

corner of it. Another day of skiing and trekking brought us to the finish line late in the afternoon. We crossed it in sixth place. Of course, I like to win, but I was proud to have accomplished something that served as a legitimate test of mental fortitude, and to complete a challenge that had halted some of the best teams in the world. I had started the race as a newcomer to international expedition racing, so much so that Karen had taken to calling me "Dennis the Menace," based on my youth, blond hair, and enthusiasm. My racing resume didn't say I was ready for Explore Sweden, but my ego told me I could do it, so I did.

Ten minutes after finishing, I fell asleep at the hotel dinner table—and this time, my teammates let me sleep.

▲▲▲

HAVING AN EGO, AS I LEARNED IN THAT RACE, IS ABSOLUTELY ESSENTIAL at times. At other times, though, the best thing you can do for yourself is to throw that ego right out the window and ask someone for help.

I had embarked for Explore Sweden a week or two after my graduation from CU. When I came back home after the expedition race, I expected to be "the guy" in Colorado endurance racing. The guy who would win the snowshoe races, the guy who could be counted on for a top-three finish in the ultradistance runs and bike rides, the guy who could help lead the adventure racing teams to victory. Instead, I returned to find myself playing second fiddle to a 26-year-old force of nature from Michigan named Josiah.

While I was in college and off in Moab and Sweden racing, Josiah Middaugh had blown into town and kicked butt. Over the coming years, as I began to try to establish myself as a professional athlete, I raced Josiah often in snowshoe races, running races, triathlons, adventure races, and multisport races of various types. I'm happy to say that I'm one of the few who have beaten him. But it didn't happen often, and, even though I always gave it my best shot and honestly believed I could beat him each time, I have finished second behind him in more than 20 races.

I was a professional runner all right: a professional runner-up to this guy!

I became obsessed with trying to figure out how to beat him. What did he eat? What kind of equipment did he use? What kind of secret workouts was he doing? Whatever it was, he was clearly doing something right and doing it often. Josiah (whose first name is pronounced "Joe-siah") was consistently producing multiple peak performances each winter and summer, winning races year-round, and always showing up sharp and fit—truly remarkable in sports where most athletes, even really good ones, can only reasonably peak once or twice a year.

Ego, as I have so recently professed, is essential, and at the time my ego told me that I could work, all by myself, to create a training plan that would generate such performances, and that this plan would in fact result in such strong performances that I would stay constantly sharp for the races, and that it would allow me to beat Josiah.

I tweaked, I adjusted, I got creative. And he still beat me.

I studied up. Got more scientific. Used more gadgets. And still he beat me.

I worked hard. Really hard. And still he beat me.

I put in the mental training. Hardened my mind. Became tougher and more gritty. And Josiah *still* beat me.

I did workouts like the following (taken directly from my training log at the time). Start in Boulder, Colorado, at midnight. Ride road bike 43 miles to Longs Peak Trailhead, climbing about 4,000 feet on the bike. Gain another 5,000 feet or so while running 7.5 miles to the top of Longs at an altitude of 14,259 feet. Summit at about 6:00 a.m. Run back to the bike at the trailhead. Get on the bike and ride another 57 miles to make it 100 on the day. Carry a full pack the whole way to add some mental training.

Josiah Middaugh (center) and I have been on many podiums together, usually with him in the top position. He took home the victor's hatchet (and biggest paycheck) after our battle at the Ultimate Mountain Challenge at the 2013 GoPro Mountain Games in Vail, Colorado. Over two days, we competed in whitewater kayaking, mountain biking, trail running, and road cycling. I'm on the left (second place) and Adam Wirth is on the right (third place). CREDIT: TRAVIS MACY

Josiah wasn't doing *this*, I thought to myself, as I lugged the stupid thing up and down the mountains.

He wasn't. But it didn't matter. Josiah still beat me.

Maybe it was the stirrings of maturity. Maybe it was just that I ran out of other options. But I realized at that point, as I nursed my wounded ego, that it was time to throw that ego out the window and ask for help.

And it's funny, what happens when you throw out your ego. As soon as you do it, previously absurd ideas become obvious solutions. That's what happened when my thinking shifted, and in a moment of clarity, I knew just who to ask for help in bringing my training to a place that would allow me to beat Josiah.

Josiah.

I realized that if I wanted to learn how to train like him, to produce such consistent performances, it made sense to learn from the guy who was doing it, week in and week out, in front of my own eyes.

Sitting there holding the phone to call Josiah and ask him to be my coach, I felt like I was in middle school, trying to get the courage to call up a cute girl, trying to think of the right things to say, hoping I would sound cool, wondering if his own ego would allow him to coach a competitor.

Josiah is ahead of the game in most areas, and this seemed to be the case here as well, because he was receptive to the idea, setting me at ease and assuring me that ego would not be a part of the puzzle for either of us.

It turned out to be a good decision on my part. Under Josiah's direction, I have been more efficient with my training, doing more with less time. His workouts make for a lot of suffering, but, hey, it's all good mental training, right? And it's made me a better athlete. In fact, my greater individual achievements have happened since he started guiding my training.

What's more, being coached by Josiah, with ego set aside, provides ongoing education for me, and I am therefore able to do an even better job with my own coaching clients.

And just in case you're wondering: since he became my coach, no, I haven't beaten Josiah. But, if I keep listening to him, I think I might sometime soon.

That could just be my ego talking.

Ultra Mindset 4: Have an Ego and Use It— Until It's Time to Put Your Ego Aside

To ME, HAVING AN EGO HAS NOTHING TO DO WITH PUSHING OTHER people around, feeling or acting entitled, or succeeding at someone else's expense—all part of the way we often think about egos. When I say have an ego, I don't mean becoming that person who "has such a huge ego!" What I do mean is telling yourself stories like this: "Through careful planning, a winning mindset, and sheer grit, I can accomplish literally anything I want to accomplish. I may fail and have to start again. It may take a long time, and it probably will not go quite as planned, but I will make it because I believe so strongly in myself and what I can do."

That night in Sweden, I told myself the story of Travis Macy's young life, how I had already persevered in a number of events that you've read about; how I had worked and trained hard to get to the point where I was even being considered, at age 22, for a slot on a top international professional adventure-racing team.

That was the ego that got me to continue that day. That's the ego required to get off the couch and start exercising, do your first 5K, or ride (or run) 100 miles. You need that ego if you want to make it through college or get a good job, start a business or become the CEO. You better have that ego if you want to keep your marriage strong or rebuild it after things fall apart. Without that ego, your chances of pulling through in the face of illness, depression, and tragedy are greatly diminished. Want your kids to love you and look up to you when they're adults? You better start with that ego as soon as the pregnancy test shows positive. The ego associated with the Ultra Mindset is a deep self-confidence rooted not in your talent and ability as much as in your work ethic and resilience—and your confidence in the idea that they will pull you through anything you face.

As with our other Ultra Mindset principles, there is science as well as experience behind this one. In his excellent book *Good to Great*, Jim Collins and his research team identify the very best of leaders as those who are insanely committed not to their ego but to their cause. They make decisions based on what will be best in terms of reaching their companies' goals and objectives, rather than what will stroke their egos, and they consider real observations instead of emotional bravado in deciding what to do. Collins calls the people who do this well "Level 5 Leaders."

I like what Collins has to say here, and I'm telling you to be your own Level 5 Leader.

Do this by developing a clear vision and a road map of what you can do in an area of life and with your time on earth as a whole, and then relinquish bravado, think objectively, and readily ask for help from friends, family, colleagues, teachers, coaches, and even your so-called competitors. Sometimes, it might mean reading a book, taking a class, or asking for help from someone who is supposedly below you in the professional hierarchy; the key is to keep learning by asking for help often. You may be making yourself vulnerable when you ask for help, and that's a great sign of progress! As described so eloquently by Brené Brown, PhD, in her 2012 book *Daring Greatly*, making yourself vulnerable—and being comfortable with that—is a fundamental element of growing, succeeding, and being happy.

Mindset 4 REFLECTION

Accomplishing big goals requires perseverance, and that requires a high view of self. The Ultra Mindset often requires taking on great challenges that, according to our resume or experience, we may have no business tackling. In such cases, belief in what you are capable of doing is your best friend. This belief in one's own capabilities is also known as "self-efficacy." Let's assess yours. Ask yourself:

What are your goals?
How will you get there?
Why do you believe in yourself? What attributes do you have that you think will help you reach your objectives?

Accomplishing big goals usually takes something else, as well: help. Nobody makes it alone. Few of us achieve anything in life without assistance or guidance from others. You'll get a lot further if you have the humility to ask for help, and sometimes it's waiting right where you might least expect it. So now it's time to put your ego aside and ask yourself *these* questions:

> *What kind of help could you use in reaching your goal?*
> *Who will you ask?*
> *How will you approach that?*

Here are my answers:

As I consider the six questions above in relation to my own life, I think primarily of goals in three realms: racing, family, and career.

Reminding myself that I have achieved significant success in racing—and more important, that the same mindset and work habits I've used in racing will also lead to results for my career and young family—makes me believe in myself. So does my sense of self-efficacy (also known as my ego).

Simultaneously, I know I must continue to ask for help around almost every corner, much like I did when calling upon Josiah as an endurance coach. I have recently started running Macy College Consulting, our independent college admissions counseling business (www.macycollegeconsulting.com), alongside my wife, Amy. Her experience in this field far surpasses mine, and I have to ask her for help almost every day.

I likewise turn constantly to other experts—notably in the area of parenting—so I can learn from their experience, wisdom, evidence, and mistakes. Finding help doesn't have to be expensive, by the way: I often listen to audiobooks on parenting from the library while I'm out running or biking. These experts may not know me, but I've asked for their help, and they have provided it.

I could go it alone with racing, family, and career, but I'm confident that asking for help will lead to better results—and a more enjoyable journey.

Mindset 4 ACTIVITY: The Kiwi "Mission"

Got a race coming up? Or maybe you're just looking for a new challenge. Here's one that will stoke your ego and get you in great mental and physical shape.

It's a concept developed by the great adventure racers of New Zealand—competitors such as multiple Adventure Racing World Champion Nathan Fa'avae and five-time Speight's Coast to Coast winner Richard Ussher (also an eight-hour Ironman finisher). They call it a "mission," a training session that combines *long-duration activity* (which could be 90 minutes or 12 hours, depending on where you are in your fitness) with an *intentional and meaningful route choice* (which could be anything from circumnavigating your local park to circumnavigating a mountain range).

A mission can be completed with one mode of travel (running, biking, kayaking, or swimming) or with any desired combination.

When: I try to do sessions like this on the weekends, with the last big outing coming two weeks before a big race. Long, unique, relatively unstructured outings can be a great mental boost if you find yourself grinding away at the same training regimen day after day.

How: My wife, Amy, and I were lucky to spend almost a year bumming around New Zealand's South Island, and I got to know some of the world's best multisport athletes there. Getting out in the bush to train hard is a way of life there, and they are always talking about going out on a "mission," which is basically an extended training day that also takes you somewhere interesting. Neat training missions can be done in the wilderness, but they can also be completed without leaving the city.

For example, I bet someone could do it in Manhattan, spending, for example, several hours in Central Park or Prospect Park, and maybe running a loop or two; then getting on the bike for another loop; then trekking through the back paths, making sure to see parts of each park that you've never seen before. (Suggestion: Find the War of 1812 fort in Central Park; and, in Prospect, climb Lookout Hill, for a grand view of the borough and a little history lesson on the Revolutionary War's Battle of Brooklyn, some of which was fought in what is now Prospect Park.)

You're in a big city, of course, and while NYC is one of the safest large cities in the country, common sense and sensible precautions should be taken.

And although I've used New York City as an example, an urban mission could be staged in any city—as well as any suburb or rural area. Bringing along a friend or two on your mission will make it even more fun.

Extra: The Kiwis never do contrived missions, and their routes are chosen with care and intent. For example, they might run from one side of a mountain range to another by climbing and descending Goat Pass, or do a big loop from hut to hut in Nelson Lakes National Park. To make your experience real and fulfilling, choose a route based more on a compelling place to go than on a specific distance or time. Personally, I enjoy riding my road bike to a trailhead and then stashing it in the woods while summiting a peak or running to a cool lake.

Mindset 4 LEARN

Josiah Middaugh

RACING LIFE

Josiah is one of the top XTERRA triathletes in the world. He excels in these off-road versions of the swim-bike-run endurance event, in which participants run on trails and ride mountain bikes. Josiah is a ten-time USA XTERRA National Champion, and he has worked very hard to get there. He hasn't lost a snowshoe race in a decade, and here in Colorado—a place where it seems like half the people you meet are training hard and going big—he's Top Dog when it comes to multi-sport racing in the mountains. Josiah coaches endurance athletes, and he's generous with his time and wisdom, even when crafting the training plans of young guys whose goal is to beat him, one of these days (see josiahmiddaugh.com).

REAL LIFE

What you see is what you get with Josiah, and I am always impressed by his quiet confidence when it comes to training, racing, coaching, and raising a family. Even though he's reached the top level in his sport, he's always looking for ways to improve. He earned a master's degree in human movement a few years ago, and he puts it into practice with his coaching and training. Josiah lives in Eagle-Vail, Colorado, and spends a lot of time in his roles as a committed husband and father of three young children.

JOSIAH'S THOUGHTS ON EGO AND ASKING FOR HELP

Several years ago I was at a crossroads with my professional racing and coaching. I was coming off of knee surgery, my wife was pregnant with our third child, and my future in elite racing was uncertain. I needed to find out for myself if there was some secret combination or sequencing of training that only a few coaches in the world knew about to reach peak performance. With a nine-month racing season, I needed a solution that allowed for multiple peak performances in a calendar year, and with a family and career I needed the most time-efficient training methods.

Applying Travis's principle of giving up your ego and asking for help, I had to admit that I didn't have all of the answers. I decided to pursue a

(continues)

master's degree in human movement at the A. T. Still University of Health Sciences in Mesa, Arizona. I jokingly call my education a master's degree in triathlon, since I decided early on to direct all of my efforts to answering as many questions as possible regarding endurance training.

A big selling point for me on this particular program was the opportunity to be a student of one of the best running coaches, and an authority on endurance training at altitude, Dr. Jack Daniels. Under his guidance, I wrote a series of papers that essentially provided the building blocks of my new training program. Among other topics, the program involved a new model of periodization and peaking, as well as new ideas on altitude training and triathlon-specific strengthening and conditioning programs, much of it based on cutting-edge research that I was exposed to through my graduate work. In short, I allowed Dr. Daniels and his colleagues to help me help myself. I'm pleased to say that putting my ego aside turned out to be a real boost to my ego! Since I completed my studies, I have won three more XTERRA Triathlon National Championships.

—Josiah

Think About Your Thinking: *What* and *Why*

LIFE MOVED ALONG QUICKLY FOR ME AFTER I WAS SAVED by my ego at Explore Sweden. The summer after graduating from CU in May 2005, I turned down a teaching position at Denver Academy, the school where my girlfriend, Amy, was working, to pursue adventure racing.

It wasn't exactly the safe, smart choice. "Professional" adventure racers don't make a ton of dough, and I didn't even have a concrete sponsorship plan or program when I turned down that first opportunity for a real job. Still, I put my head down and decided to give adventure racing a go—and in retrospect, I'm glad I did.

I competed in two more expedition races with Team SOLE, the same crew from Explore Sweden. We persevered through EcoMotion Pro in Brazil, a five-day slog through mud and rain that included a full day of mountain biking, during which two members of our four-person team rode with only one pedal because the pedals on one of the bikes broke. As you can imagine, riding a bike with one pedal is worse than trying to hop on one leg. You're not going to go too far. We worked as a team, using tow lines and pushing, to essentially pull Paul and Darren through the long mountain-biking segment.

We finished second in Desafío de los Volcanes, an expedition race in Patagonia at the remote southern tip of South America. The race started on the beach in southern Chile and continued across the country to San Martín de los Andes, a beautiful mountain town in Argentina. At one point in the middle of the night in a windy rainstorm, we came upon another team with two flipped kayaks out in a large lake. Their boats had capsized in the storm and then filled with water, preventing the four bobbing racers from turning the boats back over. The circumstances were dire, and all four of them were getting cold—and fast. Thanks mostly to the exceptional paddling of Paul and Darren, we were able to tow the other team and their boats to the shore, where they started a fire and warmed up. The team of Argentinians completed the race. They were grateful, but it was a reminder about how truly dangerous adventure racing could be. Still, looking back, I realize I was potentially putting my life on the line in these races for little more than a few bucks and some free t-shirts. This had to change—and soon it did.

Back home, a scramble of part-time substitute teaching and fill-in food services work paid my bills until Dave Mackey, Danelle Ballengee, and I secured a solid adventure-racing team sponsorship from Spyder—the same ski company that supported Bode Miller and the other top skiers for so many years. This was the adventure racing equivalent of a big Nike or Adidas sponsorship in road running. Dave and Danelle were both experienced athletes in their mid-thirties who had been making money running and adventure racing for years, and I was pleased to be in their company. I was paid $1,250 per month, a comfortable sum for a single 22-year-old to live on, and Spyder also committed to funding our team to adventure race around the world every six weeks or so. I was now making a living as a pro adventure racer, and I was stoked! We put together a very competitive team, and we wanted top results, right away.

We got them at the 2006 Raid World Series in Australia, where Team Spyder took first, despite almost being hit by a startled, rampaging emu—picture an ostrich that's a little bit smaller and just as fast—that darted out the of the bush as we rode the final few kilometers to the finish line. I've been cold, I've been tired, I've been in pain . . . but I have never been so scared in an adventure race as when I saw that thing came galloping toward me! I probably never pedaled so fast, either.

We also won stages at competitive races in Mexico, building our fitness, teamwork, navigation, and overall competitiveness.

We then geared up for the Primal Quest (PQ), America's largest and most lucrative adventure race at the time, which would happen right smack in the middle of Moab's July heat. To prepare for PQ, I entered the Kokopelli Trail Mountain Bike Race six weeks earlier. A couple hundred of us had started the unofficial, underground "race" at the Moab portal of the infamous Kokopelli Trail, and our goal was to ride as fast as possible, nonstop, to the other end of the trail near Loma, Colorado, 142 miles away. Kokopelli was a fertility deity in various American Indian cultures. The trail, which passes near numerous archaeological sites while circumnavigating canyons, valleys, and mountains, is completed by most riders over a series of three to five days with vehicle support. Our race was to be a continuous push over the whole trail, and the only rule of this unofficial event was that support was not allowed; you had to take all your food and water with you.

We started at midnight, and I crashed just a few hours into the race, shattering my clavicle and eliminating any chance of making it to Fruita on the bike. Thankfully, and luckily, this is the only time I have had to stop a solo race because of injury.

The rider behind me, who went, ironically, by the nickname "Doom," stopped to help, sacrificing his own finish. He picked up our bikes and helped me hike a few miles to a high point, where we found cell reception. Although my hypothermic shivering generated significant pain in the break site, I took in the immaculate sunrise over Fisher Valley with a surprising peace, happy to be alive and thankful for a stranger's generosity.

More painful than my shattered clavicle and wrecked shoulder was the disappointment of missing one of our key races for the year. Spyder valued our presence and performance at Primal Quest, and I had been working around the clock to prepare physically, mentally, and logistically for the race. Still, as I would discover again years later at the Ice Trail Tarentaise in France—when, as mentioned earlier, that unzipped backpack would force me to make a very tough ethical decision on the run, and in the process lose a podium finish—things in racing and life often don't go as we've planned. You just suck it up and keep trying your best regardless: so instead of racing at PQ, I spent weeks riding a stationary bike in the basement of my apartment building, pedaling along in an upright position with my left arm in a sling and my right arm hanging onto a ski pole for support. That was just about all I could do, but it was better than nothing, and sometimes doing your best is just about enough to make it through, even if it's less than ideal.

Two months later, in August 2006, with my clavicle held together by a titanium rod and a bunch of screws that are still there today, I was ready to roll with Team Spyder at the Adventure Racing World Championship (ARWC) in Sweden. The ARWC took over as a prominent international event after Mark Burnett closed shop at the Eco-Challenge in order to focus on his burgeoning television career. The Eco was the race my dad had competed in a decade earlier, so it felt good to know that a Macy was still represented in the world's top adventure race.

Like the old Eco-Challenge, the World Champs bring a true international flair to the sport. The race takes place in a different country each year, and the 2006 event in Sweden brought out the best teams in the world. Perennial champions Team Nike PowerBlast, mostly from Colorado, were the favorites, but they would surely face tough competition in squads from around the world sponsored by Merrell, Buff, and The North Face as well as Spyder. Yes, our plan was to be right in the mix from start to finish, earning a podium finish and, we hoped, the win.

Danelle was out of this race with an injury, so Dave and I teamed up with Darren Clarke, the same good-natured, hard-nosed Aussie who had prodded me awake during my moment of truth in the Explore Sweden race a year prior, and Frida Rosenberg, a tough Swede whose local knowledge would surely come in handy. Although the World Champs would not involve nearly as much snow travel as the previous year's Explore Sweden (and it was unlikely we'd need to break into another abandoned cabin), we were still way up north. We'd cross into Norway a couple of times, pass through small villages where the economy was based on reindeer farming, traverse a few big glaciers, and have the chance to see orcas while sea kayaking—though we wouldn't want to get *too* close.

Traveling to a competition like this overseas is an adventure in itself. If you've ever traveled with golf clubs or skis, you know that "extras" can be a challenge from the curb to the ticket counter. Now imagine that scenario with a 48-gallon plastic gear tub and a 48-inch bike box and a 50-pound duffel bag, each one stuffed to the gills with shoes, clothes, life jacket, paddle, energy bars, crampons, headlamps, and plenty of drink-mix powders and energy gels that may or may not set off airport security investigation procedures. The situation is rife for chaos and delay, and both are par for the course.

Dave and I encountered a "typical" adventure-racing travel experience that began with an argument at the airline ticket counter over baggage fees for bike boxes and heavy duffel bags, progressed to sprints through airports to make connections (while carrying 40-pound packs with food and gear), and culminated in searching out myriad pieces of baggage at the final destination. At one flight stop-over, just before boarding, we happened to notice a crowd gathering at the gate-side window. We joined the gawkers to see a runway bag-gage vehicle dragging a plastic bike box—yes, one of ours—that was trailing something *on fire*. The flame went out after about 10 seconds, and the subsequent rush of airport personnel to the site obscured our view. We boarded unsure of what had happened, and discovered upon arrival that a lithium-ion battery for one of our mountain bik-ing lights had popped out of the box and ignited. We'd have to get a new battery, but the bike was not damaged; nor were we rounded up and thrown into a cell for interrogation.

We arrived at the race site, a remote hotel, somewhere near the Arctic Circle, jet-lagged and spent from the journey. Resting up nicely with sleep and a stress-free environment is not exactly part of the typical adventure-racing program, and the Ultra Mindset is essential before the race as well as during. And, let's be honest: it's not just traveling to the Arctic Circle that can potentially drain you in the days leading up to a race. While it may not involve quite as much gear, traveling to New York City or Chicago to run the big marathons, dealing with long lines at number pick-up and the race expo, and managing the logistics of getting to the start line can also be draining. Even though these events are well organized, when you're dealing with 40,000 other people in the same event, not to mention a mil-lion spectators, it's just as much of a pre-race endurance test.

Wherever they're held, endurance sports are often characterized as a series of emotional peaks and valleys. Writing back in 1937, the great marathoner Clarence DeMar (seven-time winner of Boston, a feat likely never to be repeated) described well the inner roller-coaster ride of the long-distance athlete—and why he loved it. "Do most of us want life on the same calm level as a geometrical problem?" DeMar wrote in his now-forgotten classic on running, *Marathon*. "Certainly we want our pleasures more varied with both mountains and valleys of emotional joy, and marathoning furnishes just that."

Sport is, all so often, described as a microcosm of life in general. The particular undulations of endurance sports that DeMar described make it even more akin to the rhythms of the rest of our lives.

At work, you might get high when your new idea is celebrated by colleagues, and then low when it's rejected by management. In Sweden, we got high with a 1,000-foot zip line over a deep canyon, and then low when we got lost trying to find our way to the next checkpoint.

At home, you might get high through a relaxing morning with your spouse and kids, and low as the shit hits the fan when, around bedtime, the kids are overtired and everyone falls apart. In Sweden, we got high kayaking under the endless stars amid orcas in the sea, and then low the next afternoon when, still paddling, none of us could stay awake, and we floated in place for an hour, hoping we wouldn't capsize as we gave in to sleep.

In life, people get high with a wedding and a baby or a new job and good friends, with the lows of sickness, financial struggle, death, and rejection rearing their heads intermittently. In Sweden, we took off to a flying lead over the first few hours, aced an orienteering course, and engaged in deep and meaningful philosophical conversation on a hike over vast glaciers. We also lost an hour in a bike mechanical, shivered through a daylong rainstorm, and yelled at each other in a sleep-deprived stupor.

We know this: we know the inevitability of highs and lows. And yet, when we find ourselves being buffeted by these ups and downs, we often seem unprepared—we're either flushed with overconfidence—an almost unsustainable euphoria—or dashed to the rocks of depression.

Why is this? Why do we let ourselves get caught in the tides like an unprepared swimmer? Because we don't think about our *thinking*.

Thinking ahead about how you will think—how you will react—when those highs and lows come along is a key to success in both racing and life, particularly when you think about what you will be doing at a given time and why you will be doing it. This is, as we found out in Sweden, one key to a consistent balance and eventual success—or disappointing lack thereof.

Over the four days of the ARWC in Sweden, Team Spyder experienced the usual gains and setbacks. We started strong, leading the field up a ski hill in a steep, hour-long run before transitioning to a technical biking segment that covered some 20 miles of trails over about two hours. Things were going well, and we were leading the World Champs!

Circumstances changed in a flash when Frida's bike chain skipped off the rear chainring and became lodged between the drivetrain and the spokes. It's like wedging a nail in between a car's piston and the cylinder: you're not going to move unless the obstacle is removed. Dave and I worked together to wrench the chain free, but by the time we were moving again, the entire field had moved ahead of us. Alone and on a deserted trail, we restarted the race—in last place.

One good thing about long races (as in life in general), though, is that there's almost always time to battle back if you take care of yourself, stay calm and remain positive, and move efficiently. We did just that for a few days, steadily picking off teams as we took on daring zip lines, slept briefly in tents of caribou hide, sea kayaked among orcas, tackled challenging orienteering in thick woods, navigated serpentine caves with underground rivers, and trekked over glaciers and mountains. All the while, as we navigated our way through this land of natural wonders, we knew that we were slowly but surely making up for lost time.

At one point, we found ourselves taking on a long inline skating section at night. While it's not a typical adventure-racing discipline, the Swedes love their rollerblades, and this one was no skate through

Sleeping for an hour or so the middle of the day can sometimes be a good option in a long adventure race, particularly if it will be too cold at night for team members to rest well, which was generally the case in Sweden. CREDIT: TRAVIS MACY

the park. The inline skating section involved over 35 miles of hilly terrain, and at least one big climb on a dirt road that required removing your skates and running uphill in socks (unless you were smart enough to bring shoes along, which I was not). As in most other rural places around the world, ranchers in the far north of Sweden use "cattle guards" to keep their cows (or reindeer, as it were) within a given section of pasture. Where a fence between pastures crosses a road, the cattle guard, which is a three-foot-deep, eight-foot-long hole in the road covered with bars running perpendicular to the road, stops hoof traffic while allowing vehicles to pass without having to open a gate.

The cattle guards, I'm sure, are effective in reindeer containment. But these things were potential death traps for a team of adventure racers skating along at night. Hit the bars with your skates, and you are guaranteed to fly forward onto the pavement ahead as your feet stop and momentum does not. Whoever was in front would have to dive into the ditch upon sighting the bars of death in the headlamp beam! Sometimes, you're happy to finish a section of an adventure race simply because your feet, your butt, or your shoulders hurt so bad. Other times, you're glad to be done with a section because you can finally stop thinking about how it might kill you. That inline skating section was one of the latter.

The final 24 hours of a long adventure race are like the last straightaway in a mile run on the track: you're almost to the finish line, and it's time to risk it all in order to take the win. Team Spyder's homestretch began with a six-hour mountain trek that offered a variety of route choices on the way to the glacier we would later traverse. I was the team navigator, so the choice about how to get to the glacier rested on my shoulders. Should we follow the dirt road to the east on a safe but longer route? Go northeast on a trail that was marked on the map, and probably went the right way? Or go directly north, straight down a drainage that would make for the shortest route, but could also get us stuck in thick, crawl-on-your-hands-and-knees bushes, or maybe rim-rocked (slang for stuck, literally, on top of or at the base of a cliff)? I was the guy with the map, and I knew I had to pay close attention and think on my feet in order to make the right decision.

A drainage is, simply put, a place where water flows or has flowed. A small drainage could be just a groove in the hillside; a large one could be a canyon. Water likes to take (and make, through erosion) a direct path, so following our narrow drainage in the mountains of northern Sweden was definitely the shortest and possibly the fastest route. Water does, however, like to attract vegetation, and it also drops right off cliffs at times; these obstacles could potentially slow us on this route.

If I may draw another parallel between adventure racing and the rest of your life: choosing a route in one of these competitions is kind of like navigating the route you take through life. You consider where you are related to where you want to go, decide on a reasonable level of risk, do your best with whatever information you have at any given moment, commit to the direction, and try not to look back. Carefully examining the map's contour lines, vegetation boundaries, drainages, and elevation markers as we approached the point of departure for the three routes noted above, I considered the options, mulled them over briefly, and came to a decision.

"Let's go for it, guys. Down the drainage!" Perhaps not quite as stirring a battle cry as "Remember the Alamo!" but it had its desired effect. We went charging along the watery trace. The choice was risky: we would either gain an hour (because it was more direct and shorter) or lose three or more (if we ended up at the top of a cliff and had to turn around). But my teammates believed in me, and attention to detail on the map told me the shortcut was passable.

As it turned out, running down the creek *was* possible, and we threaded the needle between two cliff bands before reaching a large river at the terminus of the smaller stream we had been following. The risk had paid off! One team that had left the last transition area hours before us was now just on the other side of the river, and we were gaining ground quickly. The race was coming to a close, and it was time to go hard or go home. We took our chance, went hard, and gained some valuable time.

A buck-naked, arm-in-arm, rather-sketchy, I-probably-wouldn't-do-it-now-that-I'm-a-parent ford of a flooded and frigid glacial stream had bought us more time and another position in the field. We then moved consistently on a technical glacier trek that involved crossing shear, crevasse-laced ice while roped together for safety. The crampons attached to our mountaineering boots provided a solid connection to the world—and a barrier between life and death. We passed one team on the glacier that was about to be rescued by a helicopter, because one athlete's tender, blistered, bleeding, waterlogged feet couldn't handle another step on the steep, uneven ice.

At the commencement of the glacier trek, we transitioned to kayaking with two other teams, all in the hunt to place as high as second. *Second place in the world!* We were stoked, and we hurried through the transition, with thoughts of why we were racing—*to finish on the podium in the World Championship*—ruling our minds.

During the previous trek, when I'd forced our hand with a daring route choice, I'd been thinking hard about exactly what I was doing, zooming in on contour lines, vegetation boundaries, drainages, trails, rock features, and everything else that impacted my navigational choices. Now, as the excitement picked up and we hustled to get on the water with or ahead of other teams, my thinking shifted to our greater racing goal. I had glanced at the upcoming paddling route earlier, and I knew that all we had to do was kayak downstream until we saw the landing on the right side of the river a few hours later. Given that it's not even possible to paddle a kayak upstream in a huge, fast river like that one, I thought, how hard could it be to simply go downstream?

We transitioned quickly, and became even more enthused to know that we now held a slight advantage over two teams that paddled well. If they caught us, we could ride their draft, just like cyclists in the peloton at the Tour de France.

Four hours into a paddle that should have taken about three, Dave and I paused our conversation about how we would strategically and systematically destroy our competitors on the final two sections—a trek with caving and a 40-mile, downhill bike ride on a paved road to the finish—to talk about our progress on the current paddling section.

"Uh, shouldn't we have been there by now? How are we looking on the map? How's the compass direction?"

"What do you mean? Don't you have the map in front of you?"

Neither of us had the map out, and we each thought the other did. Once it was extracted from the cargo hold (where it clearly shouldn't have been), the map revealed that the big river we were paddling intersected a very large reservoir at one point. To get to the desired endpoint for the paddling segment, teams had to skirt one edge of the reservoir and continue along the river, heading south. In our giddy excitement about why we were racing and how close we were to the finish, we had drifted into the reservoir and paddled for about two hours to the east, 90 degrees from the correct direction.

In other words, the river we wanted to be in—and where our rival teams were now paddling toward the finish line—was two hours back in the direction we had just come from.

As you can imagine, the paddle back was quiet and tense. I tried not to attempt to read the thoughts of my teammates, since, as I had been the primary navigator for most of the race, the mistake was largely my fault. Going two hours in the wrong direction is definitely not unheard of in long adventure races, but, at least for top teams like ours, it usually doesn't happen when you are simply paddling down a river. And this was just about the worst possible time to lose four hours.

Though we were angry, we got back on course and kept racing hard. We were tough, experienced athletes, and we told each other new, positive stories to keep ourselves focused:

Teams ahead will falter.

They haven't slept enough.

By focusing very hard on exactly what we are doing all the way to the finish line, we'll avoid errors like that last one, regaining our position and making the podium.

And focus we did. It paid off on the next segment, which involved crawling and climbing through yet another flooded cave, and then hiking all night in our wetsuits, because it was so cold. We hit the final transition area at about midnight, and quickly unpacked and rebuilt our bikes for a final, 40-mile sprint to the finish.

All we had to do now was focus on the road in front of us, thinking about how to keep pedaling as we picked off a few more teams on the way to the finish. More stories:

They're going to lose focus like we did on the paddle.

If we stay alert and on task, we're going to catch them.

Simple but monotonous actions like paddling and biking on a road are extremely challenging when you are sleep-deprived. Slowly and surely over those last 40 miles, the sleep-monsters stalked us. We swallowed satchels of a nasty, black liquid that could be mixed with hot water to make coffee, taking down multiple packets at a time:

Stay awake! Keep pedaling! We can do it!

I turned to look at my teammates as we exhorted each other. When I realized that Dave was gone, I screeched on my brakes, turned around, and found that he had fallen asleep, crashed on the side of the road, and continued sleeping on the pavement. We were less than half an hour from the finish line.

What to do? Pick up my teammate and carry him? Dave is incredibly tough, but when you're so tired that you don't wake up after crashing your bike, a gentle nudge on the shoulder won't do. Dave was out. The rest of the team joined him there, and at that moment, the cold, hard, Swedish pavement felt better than a fresh bed at the Ritz Carlton. Half an hour later, I felt the freshness of the sunrise and sat up dreamily. I knew that the podium finish had now eluded us, but I was too tired to get angry. And if there was anyone to blame, it was me, for the navigational mistake on the river.

I heard a familiar voice. "Come on, mate, let's roll." It was Darren, coaxing me and my teammates to action again as he had a year ago at that truckers' outpost. "We're about to finish this race."

Thinking carefully about what you're doing is crucial on fixed-rope sections, particularly when you're sleep-deprived and carrying a heavy backpack. CREDIT: TRAVIS MACY

Ultra Mindset 5: Think About Your Thinking: *What* and *Why*

OUR MELTDOWN IN SWEDEN HAS HAUNTED ME OVER THE YEARS, AND I only recently figured out exactly how these two monumental blunders—first, paddling the wrong direction, and later, failing to hammer out what should have been a simple bike ride to the finish, when our motivation should have been its highest—occurred.

Maps errantly placed in cargo holds and insufficient sleep weren't adequate explanations. In both of those instances, we messed up, big time, in how we were *thinking*. Specifically, as described so eloquently in 2010 by Heidi Grant Halvorson, PhD, in *Succeed: How We Can Reach Our Goals*, when we should have been thinking about *what* we were doing we were thinking about *why* we were doing it, and when we should have been thinking about *why* we were doing it, we were thinking about *what* we were doing. Halvorson's excellent text, which I highly recommend to anyone who wants to set and achieve goals, summarizes findings from the latest psychological research on a variety of topics related to goals. Regarding thinking about why you are doing something versus thinking about what you are actually doing, she writes, "Think about your goals in *why* terms when you want to get energized, stay motivated, or avoid temptations. Think about your goals in *what* terms when you are dealing with something particularly difficult, unfamiliar, or anything that takes a long time to learn."

Aha! *What* I wouldn't give to have read this book before the race in 2006! Here, I learned what we did right—and where we went wrong—at the Adventure Racing World Championship in Sweden.

Our thinking was right on as we moved through the field, steadily passing other teams in the hours prior to the debacle. While paddling for 12 hours, which is monotonous and requires high motivation, we thought about *why* we were pushing hard—*to catch those teams*—and it worked. The next segment, which involved challenging and risky navigation as we headed down the drainage, was difficult and unfamiliar. My focus on *what* I was doing, with very careful reading of the map, consequently worked out very well.

But here's where we went astray: just before and during the river paddling screw-up, we should have been thinking about *what* we were doing, because the navigation was surprisingly difficult and, once again, unfamiliar. By continuing to focus on *why* we were rushing around in the transition area (so fast that we failed to even keep the map out)—*to beat the other teams to the water*—we failed to even consider *what* we were doing. The price was great.

On the final biking segment to the finish of the race, which was not difficult or unfamiliar, we shifted to focus on *what* we were doing. Unfortunately, when you are doing something boring, monotonous, and simple, and you focus on *what*, the journey becomes even more dreadful and seemingly long. This was compounded by our sheer exhaustion at this point, which dragged us down even more, because inspiration was nonexistent. Here, an intentional focus on *why—to beat a few teams as we earned a high finishing place in the world championships—*would have been much more effective than what— *pedal, stay awake, pedal, stay awake.*

Team Spyder had the potential to win a world championship. We prepared well, raced hard, stayed committed, and used plenty of positive stories and teamwork. Skill and fitness were high for all team members. Our errors in when to think *what* vs. *why*, however, resulted in a mediocre performance when push came to shove at the biggest race of the year.

It's a lesson that I would apply successfully in subsequent races. The podium finishes and wins would come my way—in part because I knew better how to think about my thinking.

Mindset 5 REFLECTION

Focused thinking regarding *what* versus *why* in appropriate situations is applicable to adventure racing, work, and just about anything else challenging and worthwhile. So let's start focusing on thinking about our thinking.

Say you're out on a walk, a run, or a bike ride, or maybe you're raking leaves or folding clothes, or doing some other relatively mindless task. Do you find your motivation, energy, and enthusiasm flagging? Well, stop and think about your thinking. Are you focused on *what* you are doing, which is probably not enjoyable? (*"I'm waxing the floor. . . . I'm painting the shed. . . . This is boring. I'm hot, I'm getting tired. I don't like this."*) How could shifting your thinking to *why* at this time to add some motivation and inspiration? (*"This floor is going to sparkle and I always feel better when the house is clean. . . . When we have the family over next weekend, I know someone's going to come into the backyard and comment on how nice it looks, in part because of this freshly painted shed. It was an eyesore!"*)

Thinking about *what* you are doing is a good idea when the task is challenging and detail oriented. Thinking about *why* you are doing it is helpful when a relatively simple task becomes boring or drawn out.

A self-assessment to help you practice thinking in more productive directions, depending on the task at hand, is provided below and continues on to the following pages.

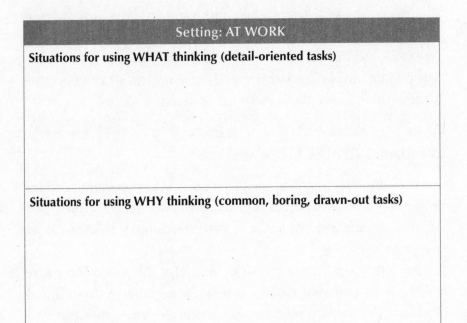

Setting: AT WORK

Situations for using WHAT thinking (detail-oriented tasks)

Situations for using WHY thinking (common, boring, drawn-out tasks)

Setting: AROUND THE HOUSE
Situations for using WHAT thinking (detail-oriented tasks)
Situations for using WHY thinking (common, boring, drawn-out tasks)

Setting: PARENTING
Situations for using WHAT thinking (detail-oriented tasks)
Situations for using WHY thinking (common, boring, drawn-out tasks)

(Table continues)

(Table continued)

Setting: ACADEMICS
Situations for using WHAT thinking (detail-oriented tasks)
Situations for using WHY thinking (common, boring, drawn out)

Setting: EXERCISE, TRAINING, AND RACING
Situations for using WHAT thinking (detail-oriented tasks)
Situations for using WHY thinking (common, boring, drawn-out tasks)

As always, I've "field-tested" these assessments for you and applied them to my own life. What I came up with is shown below and on the next page.

Setting: AT WORK
Situations for using WHAT thinking (detail-oriented tasks)
• Planning an upcoming motivational talk to ensure that it's tailored to the audience and effectively utilizes ethos, logos, and pathos
Situations for using WHY thinking (common, boring, drawn-out tasks)
• Teaching, updating the gradebook, taking attendance, and filing paperwork
Setting: AROUND THE HOUSE
Situations for using WHAT thinking (detail-oriented tasks)
• Doing taxes (once I actually sit down to do it)
• Planning a bathroom remodel, selecting supplies, and choosing contractors
Situations for using WHY thinking (common, boring, drawn-out tasks)
• Doing taxes (when trying to motivate myself to get started)
• Cleaning the dog kennel
Setting: PARENTING
Situations for using WHAT thinking (detail-oriented tasks)
• Teaching Wyatt to ride a bike
• With Amy, planning our shared parenting goals, mindsets, methodologies, and communication techniques
• Playing with Lila at the park, when I am tempted to check my phone but need to stay focused on the *what* of quality time with my daughter
Situations for using WHY thinking (common, boring, drawn-out tasks)
• Flying to Europe with a one-year-old and a three-year-old
• Getting up with kids in the middle of the night
• Keeping my cool and carrying out empathetic, consistent, and effective teaching and discipline during tantrums and sibling fights

(Table continues)

(Table continued)

Setting: ACADEMICS
Situations for using WHAT thinking (detail-oriented tasks)
• Learning a new learning management system for the delivery of my online curriculum
• Studying scientific topics related to endurance coaching, such as "functional threshold" or "VO_2 max"
Situations for using WHY thinking (common, boring, drawn out)
• Pushing hard to complete my master's degree in order to finish before Wyatt's birth
• Teaching, when my passion for the *why* is encroached upon by negative stories about low pay

Setting: EXERCISE, TRAINING, AND RACING
Situations for using WHAT thinking (detail-oriented tasks)
• Running or biking down a steep, rocky section
• Figuring out a challenging navigational scenario
• Choosing and packing gear
• Remembering to follow a nutrition and hydration protocol
Situations for using WHY thinking (common, boring, drawn-out tasks)
• Running or biking a monotonous and boring section
• Running or biking anytime I get sleepy
• Running or biking when nearing the finish line when it's crucial to go hard and leave nothing behind
• Running or biking whenever I'm going all-out and red-lining it, either in a short race or at the end of a long race

Setting: OTHER
Situations for using WHAT thinking (detail-oriented tasks)
• Studying the impacts of technology within family life and then making intentional decisions with Amy about how we will do things at our house
Situations for using WHY thinking (common, boring, drawn-out tasks)
• Going out of my way to help a stranger

Mindset 5 ACTIVITY: Technical Session

As an endurance coach, I often come across athletes who fall into a rut of doing almost the same thing for training day after day. They're thinking about the *why* ("I want to work out and get fit"), but not really taking time to consider the *what* ("In order to improve fitness, you can't always do the same workout, day after day").

One key piece that's often neglected in training is skill-specific practice.

Mental training: A challenging technical session really gets you honed in on what you're doing, and it's also a great way to escape from the general flurry of the day; if you're doing something challenging enough, you won't be able to think about that work deadline or throwing together another dinner for your ravenous teenagers.

Physical training: Developing skills, which can in many cases be differentiated from building fitness, is essential. Your mile run personal record and max wattage on the road bike don't help you much if you're trying to run or bike down a steep, rocky trail, or paddle in whitewater, or swim out in the ocean. Likewise, sports such as cross-country skiing, snowshoeing, kayaking, and swimming are all based heavily on using correct technique to move efficiently.

When: I recommend at least one technical session every week in each sport you practice. I like to do a technical session on an easier day, which often fits in well on the day before or after a harder or longer training session.

How: The night before your workout, or in the morning while you have some coffee, spend ten minutes researching or reviewing a particular skill you will practice during the technical session. Use print or online resources to learn something, and then put it into practice. Check out one video or article, and then practice one (one is better than many—just hone in on one concept), keeping in mind what you learned in your research. Remember that your goal here is to work on technique—building fitness is secondary today. Here are some skills you might work on:

Biking: On the mountain bike, focus on descending with a low body position: butt off the seat but not too far back, torso low and nearly parallel to the ground, head up and looking far ahead. Consider timing yourself for a challenging segment and then trying to improve on that a few times. On the road bike, work on a nice, smooth pedal stroke (no mashing up and down), and do some high-cadence reps of 100–110 revolutions per minute (you'll need a bike computer to track accurately) to help make a generally effective normal cadence of 90 revolutions per minute feel comfortable.

Running: For road running, work on good form and quick cadence. I recommend shooting for 22 to 23 strikes per foot every 15 seconds. You can also explore the lunge matrix, an effective ancillary workout described in detail at the website of Coach Jay Johnson, a leading expert in the running field (www.coachjayjohnson.com). For trail run-

Drafting is an important technical skill for road and mountain biking. Our teams often traveled in a paceline like this one. Here we are on a dirt road in Moab leading to the high La Sal Mountains. Credit: WWW .AXSRACING.COM / WWW.NEWCOMER PHOTO.COM

ning, work on your uphill hiking. Yes, *hiking*! Many mountain races include steep hills that can be ascended more efficiently—and just as fast or faster—by hiking instead of running, especially if you are tired. When I'm really going hard up a steep hill, I "power-hike" by bending at the back and pushing with my hands on my knees as I climb the hill; the way this technique impacts the feet, legs, and back is very different from in running, and it's a skill to be practiced.

Hiking: Spend an outing trying out options to determine your ideal pack positioning. Are you most comfortable with a tight chest strap and looser waist strap, or vice versa? How tight should your shoulder straps be? Which of the various compression straps and other features on your pack should you adjust for best fit, comfort, and efficiency?

Triathlon: Work on the transitions from swim to bike and bike to run. Use all of your race gear, and complete the transitions over and over again. If you'll be swimming with a wetsuit, practice taking it off quickly until you have it mastered. You don't want to be that guy squirming around on the ground with the wetsuit bunched up at his ankles . . . trust me, I've been there and it's not fun!

Adventure Racing: Don't forget the paddling! Learning to paddle powerfully and efficiently is essential—and it's also overlooked by many beginning adventure racers. Check out the videos at kayak product websites (for example, www.epickayaks.com) and explore the instructional resources from champion paddlers such as Greg Barton and Oscar Chalupsky. Most first-time paddlers are inclined to use only their arms in an endless series of inefficient bicep curls. Instead, use your entire torso to paddle with a smooth, twisting motion, catching the paddle in the water at your feet and exiting it before pulling back past your hips.

Extra: Other resources include excellent biking tips (www.better-ride.net), expert running advice (www.running.competitor.com), and detailed tri instruction (www.triathlon.competitor.com). I also have some skill instruction videos at www.travismacy.com.

Mindset 5 LEARN

Sam Skold

RACING LIFE

Sam is a track and cross-country runner at the United States Air Force Academy in Colorado Springs. She was an All-State runner at Evergreen High School, my alma mater, and she's tough as nails.

REAL LIFE

Sam is a driven young person who works hard with her running, academics, and military training at the Academy. She's also a typical college kid who enjoys time with family and friends, travel, and fun outdoor adventures. Sam just got a mountain bike, and she spent some time last summer tearing it up out in Moab.

SAM'S THOUGHTS ON APPLYING *WHY* THINKING

When I accepted my appointment to the United States Air Force Academy, I didn't realize I was becoming more than just a student athlete. As cliché as this sounds, I became a cadet. I didn't just have collegiate-level workouts and academics to worry about, but I also had hours of military training each week.

This piece of my life started at 0730 on June 27, 2013, when I started "Basic," the initial, intense training course that provides a mental and physical wake-up call for all Academy newbies. I soon found myself face to face with an older, aggressive male instructor who was yelling at the top of his lungs, just inches from my face, commanding me to sound off. At that moment I realized this was my reality for the next seven-plus years of my life. I didn't know what to think or do. I had no one to talk to. I was cut off from all civilization. The only thing I focused on was what I was doing. I was running and dropping to my face whenever I was told to. I was following every monotonous order, from showering in a minute's time to folding my uniforms in perfect 10-inch squares. I was miserable and had no hope of continuing.

But things changed once I realized why I was doing all this. I didn't join the US Air Force to become just a runner or just a student; I entered to show my parents what kind of a daughter they had raised. At that moment, all the yelling, mental exhaustion, and physical pain I was experiencing became bearable. I did every pull-up thinking I was showing my parents how strong I was; when I was surviving on three hours of sleep, I was showing my parents how dedicated I was; and when I wore my uniform, I thought about how proud I was making them.

Since being accepted in to the Air Force Academy, I have been occupied from 5 a.m. until midnight with military training, school, marching, and practice every day. Every second of my life has been scheduled for the next three years. At first I hated this thought. I wanted out, and I wanted to enjoy real college life and freedom, but then I remembered to think about why I was doing this to myself, and I haven't looked back since.

—Sam

The 4:30 a.m. Rule: When You Have No Choice, Anything Is Possible

IT WAS 80°F WHEN THE BOEING 747 TOUCHED DOWN on the runway of Abu Dhabi International Airport. That's typically cool December weather for a place that averages about 107°F in July.

I'd left Denver International Airport more than 22 hours earlier, just ahead of a looming snowstorm. Now I was in the desert. It was 2009, and I was flying to the United Arab Emirates to participate in the Abu Dhabi Adventure Challenge, a six-day multisport race in some of the most inspiring and unforgiving terrain on earth. For the next week, I would run, bike, paddle, swim, and climb through the vast sand dunes, deserted trails, sprawling seas, steep cliffs, and incredible cities that make Abu Dhabi a true treasure of the Middle East.

It was a different Travis Macy who walked off the plane and into Abu Dhabi's wintertime heat that morning. I wasn't the new kid on the block anymore. In fact, I wasn't a kid at all. Since our blunder at the 2006 Adventure Racing World Championships, I had matured emotionally and physically. I'd become a better paddler, a more precise navigator, and, overall, a more efficient outdoor endurance athlete. Dennis the Menace was out, and Trav was in, known to adventure racing teams around the world as a gritty competitor, solid navigator, skilled mountain biker, quick runner, and (I hoped) nice guy who played by the rules.

In 2008 and 2009, my teams had finished second at the Primal Quest, America's largest and most prestigious expedition adventure race at the time. We had won the Best of the West Adventure Race, an expedition in British Columbia and Alberta, Canada, that included endless hours of crawling over a horizontal thicket of massive, fallen trees on steep, remote mountains, and where the members of one team were awakened in the middle of the night by a wolf sniffing at their tent. I also won the Mt. Taylor Quadrathlon, a New Mexico race Dad had done when I was a toddler that involves road biking, running, skiing, and snowshoeing to the summit of 11,306-foot Mt. Taylor—and then turning around to redo all four disciplines en route to the finish. I'd also stood on the podium at the awards ceremonies for the TransMexicana Mountain Bike Race (a stage race from coast to coast across southern Mexico), the 24 Hours of Moab Mountain Bike Race (24 hours on a challenging loop in Moab), the Teva Mountain Games Ultimate Mountain Challenge (four races in two days: kayaking, trail running, mountain biking, and road biking), the KEEN Great Ocean Road Adventure Race (three days in Australia), and the Rock and Ice Ultra (140 miles of running and snowshoeing across the Canadian Northwest Territory over six days).

Amy and I got married at the top of the ski lift at Copper Mountain in Colorado. I have since raced right past the spot where we said our vows, and it's always special to go there—as well as being a good reminder that some things in life are much more important than training and racing. CREDIT: JAN DEPUY

There had been major developments in my non-racing life, as well. Amy and I had gotten married on top of a mountain in Colorado in 2008, and we moved to Evergreen in 2009, largely so I could train at altitude on the same forested, mountainous trails that had brought Dad so much fitness and peaceful solitude over the years.

Abu Dhabi was a long way from Evergreen in every sense. But this was an important opportunity for an adventure racer: the stakes here were high, with 40 coed, four-person teams from 20 countries competing for the largest cash purse in the sport. As was the case in most of the international races in this sport, the field included a disproportionate number of Kiwis. Race-hardened in the unforgiving climate and steep hills of the Southlands, the experienced athletes of Team Qasr Al Sarab and Team ADCO (who had both gained the support of local sponsors for this race) could be expected to contend for top-three finishes.

The Abu Dhabi Adventure Challenge is a descendant of the original Raid Gauloises—the event that spawned the entire sport of adventure racing—and the Gallic influence was still apparent from the number of competitive French teams that toed the line. Other familiar faces included the Swedes of Team Lundhags Adventure and the Spanish and French members of Team Buff Thermocool. Strikingly absent were the Americans of Team Nike, the most successful adventure-racing team in history. Present were an interesting new group: the Germans of Team Abu Dhabi Triathlon. Led by Faris Al-Sultan, winner of the 2005 Ironman Triathlon World Championship in Hawaii, this team of uber-triathletes generated whispers across the field and comment in the media before the race.

Would the fittest triathletes in the world have what it takes to complete a multiday adventure race? Could they win?

Tall, tan, and chiseled, they sure looked impressive in Speedos; I knew from the start that I wasn't going to beat these guys with physical superiority. But, then again, as I had learned, adventure racing is not just about physical conditioning.

My team—Salomon / Crested Butte, an amalgam of past sponsors and athletes—was prepared and ready to go. Although we had not raced together as a foursome, I had competed with each other member of the team in previous races and expected that we would work well as a team. Jon "JB" Brown and Eric "Sully" Sullivan were former competitors from the good old "Crusty Butts"—the Crested Butte team I had raced against years earlier in Moab. Since then, I had come to know them not only as talented and hardworking multisport athletes but also as good people with whom I enjoyed spending time. I spent weekends and vacations in the Gunnison and Crested Butte areas with them, learning to ski mountaineer in the winter and tackling wildflower-laden biking and running trails in the summer. JB and I made a morning run out of the Four Pass Loop, a classic, 26-mile route over four high mountain passes between Aspen and Crested Butte that most travelers take on as a three- or four-day backpacking trip. We had also made it through the 2007 Adventure Racing World Championship, a cold, wet, Scotland suffer-fest. JB and Sully were fit and ready to roll in Abu Dhabi, and the three of us were stoked to be racing with possibly the best female runner in the sport, Denise McHale.

Denise was a talented athlete and close friend from Canada's Yukon Territory. She had just won the Canadian 100K (62 miles) Road Running Championship, and had logged hours on a rowing machine to help prepare for the paddling in Abu Dhabi. She and her husband, Greg, are the kind of people who build a log cabin with their hands and hike for days to hunt wild sheep with a bow and arrow (the McHales now run their own adventure park with dogsled rides and other wilderness endeavors). Greg once held his ground when charged by an angry grizzly bear, waiting for it to get close enough that his one possible shot with a life-saving arrow would dig deep. Greg's composure (talk about mental training) paid off, and the bear was scared away by a shot to the chest. The desert was a far cry from Canada's Northwest Territory, but that didn't concern me: the McHales never complain, and they're tough as nails. I had raced with the couple in some previous races, but Greg stayed home this time because, well, it was hunting season.

Our team was fit and ready to roll, but we knew we were at a serious disadvantage. The Abu Dhabi race involved two stages of nothing but paddling, covering a distance of more than 50 miles in the ocean. It's hard to prepare for that when every body of water in your home state has been frozen solid for weeks. With such limited opportunities to train in what would be the most important discipline in this race, we knew winning the overall title could be a long shot. But that didn't mean we couldn't still win *something*. Much like Tour de France teams and riders, who seek out individual stages as targets for victory, we turned our attention to the idea of winning one or more stages in the six-day race. A stage victory in the Abu Dhabi Adventure Challenge would be big, and we knew it would be possible if we kept it together mentally and raced to our physical potential.

Many multiday adventure races start with a leisurely pace as athletes settle into a sustainable rhythm to hold over the next week. This was *not* the case in Abu Dhabi. The first day of stage racing involved an "adventure triathlon" prologue—17 total miles of swimming, biking, and running—followed by 20 miles of sea kayaking.

At the gun blast, 160 competitors shot off from the line on mountain bikes. It was an unusual sight in adventure racing: with our tires hyperinflated to speed across 7 miles of pavement (some racers even used aerobars and thin, cyclocross-style tires), we shot down the road in a daring peloton. Each racer depended on the others to hold their lines and maintain composure as we sped down the scenic beachside esplanade, pulled a hairy U-turn, and raced back to a magnificent Arabian palace for the first transition.

Ever the competitor, Jon had realized moments before the start that we would save precious time—only days later would we know how important every second truly was in this race—by cycling in our running shoes and then enjoying a seamless transition to running. The creativity paid off, and we hit the 5K road-running section at the front of the pack. As the field made its way to the palace, across a beach, and then back onto paved roads, teams jockeyed to make their presence known.

Team Qasr Al Sarab—the superstar Kiwis—shot to the front and led the way to the transition to an open-water swim.

Although long swims are standard in tris, adventure races rarely require competitors to swim half a mile in open water. But I guess this is one reason the Ironman studs were here (or maybe the course was designed to better accommodate their skills, I never found out for sure). After hurriedly stripping to our shorts and donning goggles, we dove into a picturesque bay bordering the city of Abu Dhabi. Race flags signaling the swim's finish loomed across the bay in the distance. For some racers, this swim would be a serious test. Assured by the pool training I had done in the weeks leading up to the race, I confidently fell into a rhythm in the water. When I saw the recognizable Ironman logo on the swim caps of the German squad approaching on my left, I decided to simply slide into their slipstream and draft for the remainder of the swim. It didn't work: they soared past me like torpedoes.

Having been spanked in the water, our Team Salomon / Crested Butte regrouped quickly as we transitioned to the first of a pair of 2-mile paddling sections that would sandwich a quick orienteering section on a sandy island to complete the adventure triathlon. Running in the sand dunes here provided a small taste of what would come on a much larger scale in two days' time, and most teams navigated soundly with map and compass.

Team Qasr Al Sarab took the Adventure Triathlon Prologue in a decisive victory, and we finished shortly after them. The Kona studs of Team Abu Dhabi Triathlon were not far behind, and they seemed a force to be reckoned with after the Prologue.

Still, we knew that although the Ironman distance triathlon is certainly one of the most grueling competitions on the planet, it is staged over a single day. In an adventure race like this, there were still five days to go.

After a quick beachside shower and rehydration session, racing began again that afternoon with 20 miles of sea kayaking from the city of Abu Dhabi to a small, remote island to the north. The start was "Le Mans"–style (again the French influence). That meant we would line up on foot along the beach, and on the "go" signal, all sprint through the sand to our boats sitting on the shoreline, and then clamber into the two-person sea kayaks as we chaotically launched into the water (each team of four had two kayaks, which were equipped with sails). You see this kind of start in challenges on *Survivor*, and I'm pretty sure the show's mastermind, Mark Burnett, knew these chaotic starts from his days in adventure racing, and realized they would make for good TV.

The triathletes hadn't spent a lot of time in boats, while the Kiwis had. Jon and I took the lead for the first 500 yards of paddling, leaving the Ironmen behind. But then we were passed by one of the New Zealand teams; they paddled off into the distance as if they had outboard motors on the backs of their boats. Exiting the shelter of an island after a few kilometers, we hit the swells of the open seas. For the next few hours we would paddle in open water, periodically engaging the sails to gain a boost from the wind if it blew in the right direction. The ocean rose and fell with great power, often pushing our kayaks sideways and forcing us to "surf" the swells, and we were often far enough from shore that swimming the distance in an emergency would be a great challenge. Such conditions are, needless to say, a bit unsettling for people from Colorado and northern Canada. (Snow, altitude, bears—no problem. Ocean, heat, desert—now I'm getting nervous!) At one checkpoint that required us to paddle to shore before heading back into the ocean, the waves broke on a sandbar. Most teams beached safely here, but some were not so lucky. Getting dumped by the surf makes you feel like you're in a washing machine, and when you finally pop up you have to swim like crazy to recover lost gear. Hours later, paddling to the island where the stage ended and all the teams would camp, we encountered a raging rip current just offshore. Simply making it to the beach while paddling against the equivalent of a strong downstream current was nearly impossible, and we finally jumped out of the boats and pulled them through shallow water to the island.

At day's end, our sore muscles enjoyed a night's reprieve at the tiny island. The scene was spectacular, with stars in the sky and city lights in the distance. It was a truly memorable evening of camping with friends, and we almost forgot, if just for a couple of hours, that we had come from around the world to crush each other in a grueling race in the middle of the desert.

The next morning, we pushed off at sunrise to paddle 34 miles back to Abu Dhabi city. It would take about six hours, which is a long time to sit in a sea kayak. The satellite images we used to navigate throughout the race (standard topo maps were not available for the region) depicted sandy islands laced with thick bushes and surrounded by channels ranging from very deep to quite shallow. Finding the deep water proved crucial all day, and teams that were able to move fastest through the shallows by finding slightly deeper sections excelled.

Hydration and nutrition were also paramount on the water. During this section, I drank six liters of water carried in bladders strapped to the boat deck. I also ate constantly, consuming energy bars, gels, nuts, and raisins. Salt water–saturated energy bars don't taste very good, but they still do the trick!

The Kiwi teams extended their overall lead on this long paddling section, and when we finally reached the end of the stage, the leaders had been on the beach prepping gear for the next day for quite some time. After two days of hard racing, our bodies were crushed from an inordinate amount of paddling, and we hobbled onto the bus that would take us inland to the desert for the next day's stage. We had lost enough time in two days of paddling that overtaking the Kiwis for the overall win would probably be out of the question, but we knew the running and mountain biking coming up would suit our strengths. Winning a stage in this race would be an enormous achievement, and that became our goal.

Abu Dhabi's Rub' al Khali, or "Empty Quarter," conjures images of ancient explorers, Bedouin caravans, and travelers staggering along in search of an oasis. The largest expanse of unbroken sand in the world, the area seems as desolate as the moon. Sand dunes stretch beyond the horizon, interrupted only by flat, empty salt flats. Nothing grows. There is no water. Even in the winter, temperatures hover above 100°F. Animal life is limited to a few super-adapted species that thrive under these conditions.

Such was the stage for 75 miles of running that would begin very early the next morning.

After being bussed a few hours south from the coastline, we camped in a barren flat surrounded by dunes on the edge of the Empty Quarter. Racers attacked the rich buffet of traditional Middle Eastern foods presented that evening with ravenous stomachs and smiling faces. We loaded our plates with baba ganoush, hummus, couscous, falafel, and tabbouleh. We devoured kebabs of lamb, chicken, and beef. We sipped tea while eating on our knees from low tables, and then lounged on expansive, colorful pillows brought there for the occasion. Were we twenty-first-century athletes, or nomads from another time and place? For an hour or two that night, it really didn't matter. Knowing that we would soon disappear into the Empty Quarter for up to 36 hours of daytime sun, nighttime cold, and ever-present suffering, we took pleasure in an evening of international camaraderie under traditional tents in the desert. It was like the last meal for the troops before the battle. Enjoying that cultural meal under the desert stars with hundreds of likeminded athletes is one of my fondest racing memories.

You never get enough sleep in a stage-format adventure race, because there's always gear to deal with, maps to consult, plans to be made. As I finally began to fall asleep under the desert stars, worries filled my head. I had never run such a long stage through harsh desert before, and didn't know what to expect:

Would our gaiters and Gore-Tex shoes keep the sand out?

Would we get enough water?

How hot would it be?

Would the teams that lost time on the paddling sections be able to regain precious minutes?

We came to Abu Dhabi looking for a stage win. . . . Could this grueling trek finally be that stage?

What in the world had we gotten ourselves into, anyway?

The final question was a good one, and when watch alarms began chirping around 4:30 a.m., it was clear that more than a few teams were packing not for 75 miles of desert running but for a short bus ride that would have them back at the five-star hotel for a few days of fine drinks by the pool. Here at the point of no return—the edge of the Empty Quarter—some teams had decided to return. I couldn't blame them. Winning the whole race was probably out of the question for us at this point, as we had lost hours on the leaders during the two long paddles. To add to our worries, the race organizers had announced the previous night that each team would only get a limited number of water bottles at each of three resupply points out in the dunes. They could only transport so many cases to the remote locations, and this also ensured that teams behind the leaders would get water.

We calculated that we would get enough water to survive the trek, but that we'd be very dehydrated by the end of our time out there.

What a relief. So at least I wouldn't die from thirst and have my carcass picked at by vultures in the middle of the desert.

Needless to say, the bus to the hotel was looking pretty good at that point.

It was then that I thought about my dad. As had often happened during my racing career, at some point or another I found myself being reminded of a lesson learned from my childhood years of watching him compete, or riding my bike with him through the hills around our home, or talking to his friends.

What I remembered that morning in the darkness of the Empty Quarter—looking at the flashing alarm on my race watch—was Dad's "4:30 a.m. Rule."

When Mark Macy was about as old as I am now, he had two little kids, Katelyn and me, and he was working hard building his career as an attorney. This was also about the time he began running and biking and entering races, which soon led to the ultra-endurance competitions, such as the Leadville 100 and the Eco-Challenge Adventure Race. Training for and competing in such races was at odds with Dad's primary commitments as a family man and a professional. But as a man who wanted to live his life to the fullest, and excel in every phase of it, he was determined to somehow make it all work. He figured out how: Dad knew that one of the best times to get work done was early in the morning. While others slept, or groggily eased into their day, Dad decided that he was going to get things done.

By waking up every day before 4:30 a.m., Dad was able to get to the office, put in the time there, head out for his lunchtime run, return to work for a few hours, stop at a trailhead on the way home for a mountain bike ride, and get home in time to be with us and attend all of our afterschool events.

At age 61, I should add, Dad is still on the same program, except that he's now moved it up to 4:00 a.m. (and often earlier). He's there for every important moment of his grandchildren's lives, and still never misses my races. Unbelievable. I'm impressed.

Dad and his 4:30 a.m. ways entered my mind out there in the dark in the desert. It was indeed 4:30—and we were faced with a choice. Quit, congratulate ourselves on a good effort, and get on the bus to comfort. Or, use this early-morning rising time as an opportunity to recommit as a team, and as a springboard to a new day where we would outwork everyone else, outhustle everyone else, and out-heart everyone else, taking a chance at greatness in our sport, and an achievement we could be proud of for the rest of our lives.

"It's going to be a good morning, guys," I said to my teammates, when we'd made the turn from our camp to the starting line, and away from the air-conditioned bus that was idling nearby.

This stage was a 75-mile trek on foot through desert sand dunes. Eager to capitalize on our running backgrounds and take advantage of the fitness we'd gained by training at altitude, Team Salomon / Crested Butte moved quickly to the front of the pack. We were running, but exactly

After heeding the 4:30 a.m. Rule, I was fired up and ready to lead the pack at the start of our long run in the desert. CREDIT: WOUTER KINGMA

where were we running to? In typical road races, you have directional signs or mile markers. Not here. My teammates were counting on me to help point us in the right direction. As we jogged, slid, and climbed along, I had to navigate the unfamiliar terrain, where ever-shifting sand dunes made reliable mapmaking almost impossible. In previous races, I could use mountains, valleys, rivers, and vegetation boundaries to develop a sense of place. Out here, the only thing visible was a seemingly infinite expanse of sand, reshaping itself with each caress of the wind. Conditions were challenging, to say the least, but I was enthused by the similarity of running in deep sand to running in snow; I kept telling myself, "Trav, this is your wheelhouse." And the story worked.

Because of the real possibility of becoming irrevocably lost in the desert, organizers had permitted GPS navigation, something typically not allowed in adventure races (what's the fun of navigating when you can just let a satellite do it for you?). But here in the middle of the desert, my GPS unit's battery had died. We quite possibly could have followed suit, if I hadn't been able to use map and compass—old-school navigation tools—to get us in the right direction.

Although the dunes are constantly shifting in exact location due to wind and erosion, the salt flats remain roughly in the same place over time. As such, I would get us to a known salt flat and then take a bearing to the next one, which could be a few miles away. In between lay sand dunes, and the ridges on the dunes were the fastest way to travel. So I'd match my bearing with the ridgelines that seemed to go in the best general direction and continue to check my bearing—and generally hope for the best—as we progressed to the next salt flat.

We were in business. Or so I thought. A few minutes after I'd gotten us pointed in the right direction, Jon pointed to his feet. "Man, my shoes are too small!" As most distance runners know, your feet swell over the course of long runs. But what made it even worse for Jon was

Out in the "Empty Quarter" in Abu Dhabi, we traveled fastest by following the ridge-lines on the tops of sand dunes. It was awesome! CREDIT: WOUTER KINGMA

Trying circumstances forge solid friendships. Jon (left) and I became close comrades over our years of racing together around the world. He seemed to like me even after I drilled through his toenail out in the middle of the Sahara! Here we are celebrating a finish line in China. CREDIT: CHINESE MOUNTAINEERING ASSOCIATION

that his already tight shoes had been made even tighter by sand working its way into the spaces between the layers of fabric. What could we do? There was no Foot Locker store or Nike outlet in the middle of the Empty Quarter. Jon was just going to have to hang in there—which he did, as his toes smashed and mashed against the fabric.

Despite his heroic efforts, Jon's foot problems slowed us down. We stopped for a few minutes to address the situation. Now it was time for me to shift from the role of navigator to field surgeon: hoping to alleviate some of the excruciating pressure building under Jon's big toenail, he and I drilled through it from the top using a knife and safety pin. JB had made the choice to give up choice early that morning, and if sitting there while I drilled through his toenail in order to puncture the under-nail blister was what he had to do to keep going, he was all in. Moments later, we ran back into the dunes, knowing that we would not stop again for many hours.

As night arrived, teams continued zig-zagging, following compass bearings to nowhere under a vibrant, starlit sky. The navigation process became increasingly challenging as darkness and sleep deprivation came into play, but thankfully, I was able to remain focused on the details, thinking about *what* I was doing (as opposed to *why*) in order to stay sharp and in the game. When we stopped for our mandatory, 90-minute rest during the middle of the night, we remained almost half an hour behind the lead group, which included the Kiwis.

I heard that the Ironman team had dropped far behind. These were some of the best endurance athletes in the world: swimming 2.4 miles in the ocean, biking 112 miles down Hawaii's legendary Queen K highway, and running 26.2 miles through lava fields—they could do that better than anyone else in the world. But six days in the desert had defeated them. Like the Navy SEAL and military teams in the old Eco-Challenge, the lesson was that fitness was a necessary but not sufficient condition for completing an event like this—one contested over a number of days and involving various disciplines, not all of them, in the strictest sense, endurance events—in extreme environments.

Sunrise brought fire in the sky and timeless panorama: *Were we really adventure racers, or stranded travelers from days long ago?* On the horizon ahead, what I at first thought was another team materialized into a mother camel with its newborn. Slimy and grey with umbilical cord still attached, the baby wobbled on unsure legs while its mother observed us suspiciously. "Oh yeah, this is why I do these races," I thought silently to myself, too tired for conversation.

Moments later, with Jon pushing the pace, we caught the lead group of six teams. Our dream of winning one stage of the world's greatest adventure stage race was now a possibility. The race was on!

Summiting the final dune, with 75 miles and 19 hours of running under our belts, we spotted the finish line. To get there, we would have to drop about 200 feet down a near-vertical sand dune and then run 150 yards across a salt flat. As seven teams took off in an all-out sprint,

I channeled my old coach from the Evergreen High School basketball team. "Come on, Trav," Coach Haebe yelled in my mind. "*This* is the time to go hard!"

This time my opponent was not a towering player from a rival team; nor was I at the wrong end of a mismatch. I was strong, I was fit, and I had a lot of 4:30 days under my belt. Plus, I had a group of teammates who were every bit as determined as I was. The four of us went flying over that salt flat—Denise attached to me precariously by a tight, thin tow line (legal in adventure racing).

The finish line—a single inflated arch out in the middle of nowhere in the Sahara—was close. We dug deep, as I occasionally cast side-to-side glances at the other teams. We were a few feet ahead; then a few yards; and finally . . . we were crossing the line. Team Salomon / Crested Butte had won the stage. The 4:30 a.m. Rule had paid off, as it always does, and thinking about that stage win still brings a smile to my face.

Ultra Mindset 6: The 4:30 a.m. Rule: When You Have No Choice, Anything Is Possible

THE 4:30 A.M. RULE IS NOT JUST ABOUT WAKING UP EARLY TO GET more in during the day—as Dad did. That's part of it, of course, but there's something deeper here. The point of this mindset, simply put, is that when you have committed to something ahead of time, you don't worry about whether or not you actually feel like taking action when it's time to spring into action.

When the alarm goes off at 4:30 a.m., you must get up and get going, even—and especially—when you feel like rolling over and going back to sleep. The rule does not have to be taken literally; getting up at 4:30 a.m. is just an example of the kind of stick-to-itiveness it takes to succeed. The rule you apply to your own situation may be slightly different, or may involve doing a particular thing at some other time of the day or at some specific time each week. The point is, you make a prior commitment to yourself, and in doing so make the choice to give up choice.

Committing to something—a training program, a project, a job, a relationship, caring for a child—is one of the most important things you can do in life. This is where it starts. By committing to 4:30 a.m., literally or figuratively, you have relinquished the other options. Getting up at a time when few others do can be a first step toward achieving the goal.

Admittedly, there are a few people who bounce out of bed, bright eyed and bushy tailed, at such an early time. The 4:30 a.m. Rule is not really aimed at those people. If you're like most of us, you'd rather stay in bed. That's the point: once you've committed to the rule, you get up anyway. This mindset is about obviating any deviation from the path to your goal, just as my team and I did in the desert, when we took the path to the start line of the final stage of the race, instead of the path to the bus back to the hotel. Once we did that, there was no turning back. Nothing—not the directionless desert, not our fatigue from many days of racing, not the daunting prospect of performing field surgery on Jon's toenail—was going to stop us.

Even though, during each moment of that long day in the sun, we still would have rather been on the bus. (Until we crossed the finish line in first place, of course.)

Committing like this, and not listening to what you feel like doing in the heat of the moment, makes a monumental difference in what you can achieve. Are you going to feel like getting out of bed to go for a run, or to write your research paper, or to prep for the GRE or the MCATs, or create the website for your new business? I know I don't. But if you really want to reach something big, you are going to have to value your long-term commitment and goal more than you value what you feel like doing at any given moment.

It works for Dad, it works for me, and it works for the successful athletes, professionals, parents, and other people I know who sometimes find themselves burning the candle at both ends. When you think about it, that's a small price to pay for making the most of one's life.

The 4:30 a.m. Rule is also good for developing a commendable characteristic that's become a hot topic in academia and education: grit, defined by Webster's as "stubborn courage, pluck, determination." Angela Lee Duckworth, PhD, of the Positive Psychology Center and the Duckworth Lab at the University of Pennsylvania, studies grit and self-control, and her research suggests that these two personality traits are critical for success. Duckworth has found that grit predicts a dizzying array of achievements, including surviving the first summer of training at the US Military Academy at West Point; reaching the final rounds of the National Spelling Bee; remaining in the US Special Forces or continuing as a novice teacher; graduating from Chicago's public high schools and performing well on standardized tests; and staying physically fit. She has noted that "grit correlates with lifetime educational attainment and, inversely, lifetime career changes and divorce."

What cadets, inner-city scholars, Navy SEALs, and Spelling Bee champs teach us is that grit is essential if you want to do anything big and important. As we have already discussed, even if most steps in your big, important journey are intrinsically enjoyable, some parts are not going to be fun. Committing ahead of time and then remembering the 4:30 a.m. Rule, especially when push comes to shove and you feel like quitting, will get you through the rough spots. Pushing through, in turn, refines your grit, making you even tougher and more prepared next time around.

And we're not just talking about success in endurance sports or business or other professional pursuits. Scott Stanley, PhD, who conducts marriage research at the University of Denver, also writes extensively about the power of an intentional, deep commitment, which is really the essence of the 4:30 a.m. Rule. Stanley's 2005 book, *The Power of Commitment: A Guide to Active, Lifelong Love*, professes the value of planning, discussing, and sticking to a commitment, including a five-step, research-based plan for doing just that. His blog (slidingvsdeciding.blogspot.com) talks about, among other subjects, the value of deciding to do something in a thoughtful manner, rather than simply sliding into whatever seems natural.

So, yes, the 4:30 a.m. Rule can be applied to your marriage or personal relationships as well (although I'm not necessarily recommending that you wake your spouse up at 4:30 tomorrow morning to share this bit of insight). And I do want to be clear that you don't have to actually wake up at 4:30 a.m. every day—or even *any* day—to embrace this principle. The key idea here is to remove the possibility of quitting in the moment because you have already committed ahead of time. Your 4:30 a.m. time may come at 10:00 p.m. on a Friday night when you are in the shed tying some flies because an epic salmon trip in Alaska is your dream, or at noon

Task I Want to Accomplish	Why This Is Important	Why It's Hard to Do in the Moment
Lifting weights three days each week	Upper body strength is crucial to my racing goals.	I'm usually fatigued from running and biking, and lifting can sometimes seem like one more thing to do, especially if it's encroaching on family time.
Using simple Love and Logic (loveandlogic.com, a parenting system based on choice and natural consequences*) when helping my kids deal with tantrums, sibling nagging, and other challenges.	Amy and I believe the Love and Logic system helps kids develop grit, maturity, and resilience.	It's a lot easier to get angry and let my own stress level rise than it is to keep cool and measured, wisely following the system under the pressure of two screaming little kids.

*I have no connection to or affiliation with Love and Logic, but it's a system I value and recommend to others.

on a Sunday when you're starting a challenging conversation with your spouse that's been on your mind for a while, but that's tough to ever get started. If you're like me, though, and you kind of like the early stuff, you might think about getting up sometime in the 4:00s every week or two to see what it does for your outlook and output.

Your life, your rhythms, your work schedule—all these will influence when and how you will apply this principle. Anytime is a good time to start committing to the things you really want in life.

Mindset 6 REFLECTION

Plan ahead to achieve results at your 4:30 a.m. moment by filling in the table on pages 170–171. A few of mine are shown below.

How I Will Commit Now and Follow Through When I Don't Feel Like It (including what I will tell myself when the going gets tough)	How I Will Stay Accountable
I made a rule: "I lift weights on Tuesday, Thursday, and Sunday." So, if one of those days rolls around, I just go to the garage, turn on a little Sons of Anarchy on Netflix, and start lifting!	I use a web-based training log through TrainingPeaks. com, and I know my coach, Josiah, is watching.
I commit ahead of time in clear, intentional conversation with my wife, Amy. In the moment, I recall simple principles of the Love and Logic system, such as give them choices and use a key word to signal a mistake in behavior.	I rely on Amy by communicating with her and asking her advice.

Task I Want to Accomplish	Why This Is Important	Why It's Hard to Do in the Moment

How I Will Commit Now and Follow Through When I Don't Feel Like It (including what I will tell myself when the going gets tough)	How I Will Stay Accountable

Mindset 6 ACTIVITY: Sunrise Run

Getting up early can be difficult when the alarm goes off, but the resulting sense of well-being for the remainder of your day is more than worth the cost!

Mental growth: Practice committing to something uncomfortable ahead of time and then following through. Pay attention to how doing this changes your perspective on the upcoming day.

Physical growth: Do something that involves aerobic fitness and mimicks race-day preparation to eliminate the "shock" of an early start.

When: Do this exercise at least once a month, and up to five days a week if it will help you reach your own specific goals.

How: The night before, grind your coffee for the morning, lay out your running clothes, get in bed early, set the alarm for 4:30, and go to sleep. When the alarm goes off, no snoozing allowed (let the coffee be your inspiration, if needed)! Sneak out of the room quietly to avoid waking your spouse, and (if your house is like mine) slide across the floor to eliminate the squeaks and creaks that will wake the kids. Turn on the coffee, and get dressed while it brews. Drink some water and have an energy bar or a banana. Head out the door and run for 50 to 120 minutes on your terrain of choice at a moderate effort as the sun rises. If you can see the sun poking over the horizon, stop to enjoy it.

Extra: For safety and for motivational reasons, meet a training partner for the run. Knowing someone is depending on you will make it easier to get going. Whether you're running alone or with a partner, make sure you wear reflective clothing and practice basic safety procedures (like running with your dog and wearing a really bright headlamp for mountain lion protection, if you're running where I do).

Mindset 6 LEARN

Pam Smith

RACING LIFE

Pam spent time running cross-country, track, and road races as a young person, but she found herself out of shape after having kids. She decided in January 2008 to get back into running, and she has since excelled in ultra distances, completing over 50 races that were longer than a marathon and winning a number of them, including prestigious events like the Western States 100, the Miwok 100K, and the American River 50. Pam also blogs about her experiences (see theturtlepath.blogspot.com).

REAL LIFE

The youngest person to graduate from Temple Medical School, Pam works as a pathologist. She lives in Salem, Oregon, and is the proud mother of two kids.

PAM'S THOUGHTS ON THE 4:30 A.M. RULE

As a mom, I think ultrarunning models many of the life skills I hope to teach my two kids—things like determination, perseverance, goal setting, pushing your boundaries, and working hard. I also hope they see the joy and the passion that I have for being active and getting outside. Yes, I run because I love it, but ultimately, I hope my running influences my kids to think big and to pursue their dreams, too. And knowing my kids are proud of me (at least until they hit their teenage years!) feels great.

In 2010, I lost sight of the impact my running was having on my kids during the Angeles Crest 100-mile race. The day was hot, I was tired, and my knee started hurting. I got to a point where I didn't care anymore and I dropped out. Certainly there are good reasons not to finish a race, but that night, when my five-year-old daughter, Megan, asked, "Mommy, why did you drop out?" I didn't have one. The next morning, when she looked at me with her big eyes and said, "Mommy, you should have finished the race," it felt like a dagger to the heart. I vowed to give my best efforts to get to the finish line from then on.

I certainly didn't want a repeat of that experience in future races. For the Western States Endurance Run in 2013, I trained harder than ever. I became very regimented with my nutrition, and I picked apart every little

(continues)

Mindset 6 LEARN *(continued)*

detail to have a rock-solid race plan. Without making the 4:30 a.m. Rule an integral component of my daily plan and overall mindset, there's no way I could have simultaneously pursued parenting, my work as a pathologist, and training at an elite level.

All of these elements came together for a magical race, and I ended up winning by more than 40 minutes. Megan (now eight), joined me for the final 250 meters on the track. Sharing that finish with her was one of the proudest and most memorable moments of my life. It was a triumph after adversity, and I hope the memory and the lesson stay with her for a lifetime, too.

—Pam

Bad Stories, Good Stories: The Ones You Tell Yourself Make All the Difference

A FEW MONTHS BEFORE OUR ABU DHABI SAND-DUNE adventure in 2009, Amy and I moved back to Evergreen, anticipating raising our kids in the same lodgepole pine forests and close-knit community I had loved so much. I smiled widely as I imagined hammering the hills on bike and foot with my own children someday, just as my dad had done with me. Two years later, following a long and nerve-wracking drive to Denver during a midnight blizzard on New Year's Eve, our son, Wyatt, was born. When I was growing up, Coach Haebe, who had young children at the time, had told our team, "Guys, you can't even imagine the love you have for your own kids. You are changed forever, and your focus in life is altered." He was right, and I was stoked to be a dad!

When Wyatt was a few days old, we took some humorous newborn photos of him surrounded by backpacks, helmets, crampons, water bottles, snowshoes, race numbers, and other racing items. He seemed to be right at home.

Home was also where I knew that I needed to be, at least for a while. As a husband and a dad, I realized the footloose life of the adventure racer was going to be more difficult to maintain. Unlike some of my teammates, I wouldn't be able to just pull up stakes and jet off to some remote corner of the world quite as easily. And admittedly, there were some doubts and frustrations creeping into my generally sunny outlook. My team had twice finished fourth in prominent adventure races in China. Big disappointments. We had a talented team, we were experienced, and we had gone into those races—the Wulong Mountain Quest and the Ordos Adventure Challenge—confident that we were podium material.

Coming off those races, I found myself wondering about my own role in the subpar finishes for our team. Could I have navigated better? Pushed the pace harder at certain key moments? Provided better leadership? Trained harder for paddling, so we could have stayed closer to the Kiwis and other top teams?

Meanwhile, I was feeling somewhat stuck in my non-racing profession, teaching. A couple of years after college, and with Amy's encouragement—she had seen something in me that maybe I didn't know I had—I had applied for a job teaching English at a private high school where she already worked. I entered the classroom in 2007 and was immediately fulfilled and energized by the challenge of teaching and the potential it provided to make a significant impact. I had thought of Coach Haebe often over the years and the impression he had left on me in the classroom and on the basketball court, and a few years later, having earned a master's in education, I found myself teaching down the hallway from him at Evergreen High School and helping out periodically as a volunteer track coach on the team he was now coaching in the spring. That was all good, but I was also struggling to support my family and pay the mortgage on the teaching income. I found myself complaining, sometimes aloud, but more often (and with more impact) in my own head, about the fact that, thanks to the recession, my salary, like those of all the other teachers in Jefferson County, had now been frozen for three years. This idea seeped into my consciousness, and it somehow compounded the negative thoughts I was having about the finishes in China.

While thrilled about parenthood, I found myself brooding over the other aspects of my life. All the elements, all the characters, were now in place for a very negative scenario.

Start with those disappointing races. Throw in the meager sponsorship opportunities as a result of outdoor companies getting hit hard in the economic downturn—I was now without a financial sponsor for the first time since college. Add in the salary freeze at my full-time job. Include the pressure of being a provider and a good dad—not only to one, but soon, to two children (our daughter was on the way, due shortly after Wyatt's second birthday!).

And for good measure, toss in the angst of turning 30: that Great Divide in life.

Yes, indeed, the elements were all there for a sad story: "The End of Travis Macy's Racing Career."

I could almost see it unfolding on the page or in the movie in my mind. And I began to tell the story to myself. Excited as I was for our second child, I began to convince myself that our new addition might somehow be the straw that broke my elite-level ultra-endurance racing camel's back, as it were. Taking care of one baby had been hard enough, and now I would be doing it while also raising a little kid who was full of energy and deserved nothing but my best.

Basically, conditions were perfect for the seeding and quick growth of this overarching, negative story that quickly began to brutalize me on a daily basis:

I've got two kids and I'm 30 years old. It's going to be impossible to continue racing at a high level, and I might as well pack it up, get a regular, 9-to-5 job, and try to make some money in a corporate gig I don't really care about instead of doing something that makes a difference but not much money (teaching) and something I really care about and makes even less money (racing).

The story was strong. It pulled me down. It almost became a belief.

Thankfully, somewhere deep inside, my mental training was kicking in. Something was hanging on to my core identity, and racing was—and remains—part of that.

I realized that while team adventure racing in multiday events might no longer be the best fit for me, that didn't preclude the pursuit of a solo racing career: multiday stage races and 24-hour mountain-bike races; multiday, multisport, one-person competitions; one-day mountain-biking and ultra/mountain/trail running races; continued snowshoeing in the winter; and even the occasional ski mountaineering race (a discipline involving the use of climbing skins—that is, fabric treads for skis—to ascend slopes, and then skiing down alpine style). All of these types of races were available to me. Many such events were held in Colorado—and other places a lot more accessible than China or Abu Dhabi. Although they weren't going to make me rich, there was some money to be made at some of these events.

But was I up to doing this? I had loved the shared sacrifice and suffering—and (usually) success—of team adventure racing. Could I now become a lone wolf? I knew I could be competitive, but would I be able to handle the long miles of running, or biking, or snowshoeing, or whatever-ing, without a team, and—given the pressures of my teaching and parenting schedule—maybe even without training partners for company?

I needed to test that. I needed a goal to find out. I needed a plotline for my new story. And as I thought long and hard about the story I wanted to write during my cold and snowy winter runs in late 2012, a new and better story began to materialize. Winter in the Rockies can be harsh and unrelenting, and maybe that's why I was thinking about the desert.

Whatever the goal, I knew that it needed to be one that I pursued on my own. My new responsibilities as homeowner, dad, husband, and teacher precluded a trip to some far corner of the world with a team.

Three letters came to my mind: FKT.

Running for time on established routes to set a new "Fastest Known Time," or FKT, is a growing trend in the ultra trail running scene. Chasing an FKT appeals to adventurous runners like me because it's generally done alone or with just one other runner, and by definition is done outside of the confines of an organized race. FKT running can occur in national parks and other inspiring wilderness areas where organized racing is not permitted, and it allows a runner to pursue a meaningful course in a special place. Elite runners "race" these courses alone to set new FKT records—for example, they may run back and forth across the Grand Canyon (current record 6 hours, 21 minutes), or around Colorado's Four Pass Loop (4 hours, 27 minutes), or along the length of the Colorado Trail (8 days, 7 hours, 40 minutes), whereas non-elites find simply completing such routes to be fun and fulfilling. FKTs can be tracked and shared for legitimacy these days with GPS watches and other tech tools, and I'm a big fan of the movement. If running a certain route is appealing to you and you can do it within a reasonable degree of risk, then why not go for it?

Musing on the possibility of where to attempt such an FKT—and still dealing with my inner struggles—I began reading Edward Abbey's 1968 classic of outdoor writing, *Desert Solitaire: A Season in the Wilderness*. The book traces Abbey's time as a park ranger in Moab. "This is the most beautiful place on earth," he wrote. "The canyonlands. The slickrock desert. The red dust and the burnt cliffs and the lonely sky— all that which lies beyond the end of the roads."

Zion really is a gem of the American West. The harsh conditions and big climbs and descents make it an attractive place for an adventure. A runner here needs to have a broad range of skills and the ability to be self-reliant. CREDIT: TRAVIS MACY

A Southwest running adventure sounded like a nice awakening for me as I trudged through the winter. Abbey was writing specifically about Moab, but I had already raced there. There was also, of course, the Grand Canyon, but that route had become excessively crowded by hikers, pack mules carrying luggage for tourists, and ultrarunners like myself.

I took out a map, examined the deserts of the Southwest, and there it was: Zion National Park, in the southwestern corner of Utah. Not as famous as the Grand Canyon is for tourists, or Moab is for adrenaline junkies, Zion is no less aesthetically impressive and genuinely wild; it's a true gem of the American West. Furthermore, a close look at the map revealed that much of Zion's 232 square miles was exceptionally inaccessible, with roads few and far between and vast stretches of wilderness visited only by backpackers who carried gear for multiple days—or runners experienced and fit enough to move through them with high efficiency. Another thing that caught my eye: the park encompassed a wide range of terrain and elevations, from 3,700 feet to over 8,700 feet above sea level.

Could I run all the way across Zion in a single push? I wondered. Yes, said the Internet, which turned out to be much less profound than Abbey, albeit a bit more informative. I learned that people had been hoofing it along a network of trails running the length of Zion since the park was established. Most travelers completed the trek over the course of five to seven days, carrying heavy packs and camping along the way. In the early 1990s, the pace picked up: some of the ultrarunners of Dad's generation had started running it in a single day, calling the 48-mile journey the "Far Far Fest" and completing it in 14 or 15 hours. Over the next two decades, many male and female runners set out to run the route for speed, and the record at the time I was doing my research was 7 hours, 48 minutes, by elite ultrarunner Luke Nelson.

I had never been to Zion, but it was impressive (and intimidating) on paper. I needed a goal. I had to prove myself to myself and rewrite my narrative. What better way to do it than running across Zion National Park faster than anyone had ever done it before?

In December 2012, I set a goal to establish a new FKT for running 48 miles across the wilderness of Zion National Park. Doing so would require a lot of training. Doing so would require mental toughness and grit. Doing so, most importantly, would prove to me that, even as a father of two (one of whom would be less than two months old at the time of the run), I could train and compete as a world-class athlete.

Shortly after that, Vitargo came on as a supportive sponsor, and I had the funding and fuel I needed to fight my demons by pursuing some big goals. By forging ahead both as a working father and serious athlete, I felt I might pursue another ideal introduced by Abbey in the

Amy, Wyatt, and Lila mean the world to me. In Zion, I wanted to rewrite my story to show that competing at a high level was compatible with giving my family time and love. CREDIT: MACY FAMILY

same text: "Balance, that's the secret," he wrote. "Moderate extremism. The best of both worlds."

On April 6, 2013, I arrived in Utah sleep deprived and a bit strung out (though also overjoyed) since the birth of our daughter, Lila, seven weeks earlier. When I set out from the Lee Pass Trailhead on the west side of Zion National Park early in the morning, I was racing against much more than the current record for the run. I was racing to rewrite the negative story that had taken over my life. And I had to win.

I was entering a realm of natural beauty that some say is unparalleled, even among the natural splendors of the American West. "Nothing can exceed the wondrous beauty of Zion," wrote the geologist Clarence Dutton, one of the area's earlier explorers, in 1880. "In the nobility and beauty of the sculptures, there is no comparison."

While native people are believed to have sought out water in what is now Zion as early as AD 500, it was not until the 1850s that any permanent settlers came into this area. One of the first was a group of explorers from the Church of Jesus Christ of Latter-day Saints— the Mormons. The leader of the party, dispatched by church leader Brigham Young from the group's new settlements in the northern part of what is now Utah, was a man who would become notorious: Nephi Johnson, who had migrated to Utah in 1848. Johnson's party would explore as far west as Death Valley. He would later be implicated in a massacre of non-Mormon settlers, including women and children, in what would become known as the Mountain Meadows Massacre, but his earlier expedition prompted some of Young's followers to settle around the area that has now become the park. It was one of the first of those settlers, a man named Isaac Behuin, who is credited with giving the area its name. "These great mountains are natural temples of God," Behuin is supposed to have said. "We can worship here as well as in the man-made temples in Zion, the biblical heavenly 'City of God.'"

Others followed, including geologists and naturalists. All echoed Dutton in their proclamation of the area's beauty. In 1919, it was designated Zion National Park by President Woodrow Wilson.

Running across Zion is a fairly simple concept, and a glance at a park map reveals a clear route of established trails connecting Lee Pass on the west side to the East Rim Trailhead on the east. Like other such endeavors, however, the devil is in the details. The route climbs some 10,000 vertical feet. Gradients range from flat to super-steep, both uphill and down. Footing includes both decent trails and pavement, but most of the route is sand, rock, mud, slickrock, and riverbed. A few potential bailout points exist, but much of the route is reasonably remote, uncovered by cell service, and bereft of people—as it should be.

There was a potential pothole in my plans: a young, soft-spoken superstar named Kilian Jornet. Some of the top runners in the world (and even some of their sponsors) had picked up on the FKT trend, and Kilian is the undisputed top dog here. Born in 1987 in Spain's mountainous Catalonia region, Kilian has become the international king of ultrarunning, mountain running, and ski mountaineering. His numerous wins in organized races, including the Ultra Trail du Mont Blanc (104 miles, 31,500 vertical feet of climbing, France), the Hardrock 100 (100 miles, 33,992 feet of climbing, Colorado), and the Western States 100 (100 miles, 18,000 feet of climbing, California)—just to name a few—are unparalleled in trail running over the past decade. Possibly more impressive—and boundary-pushing—though, are Jornet's FKT projects. In 2010, he ran 23 miles to the summit of Mt. Kilimanjaro at 19,341 feet in 5 hours, 23 minutes; most people complete this trek over a number of days with mountain guides. But he also races solo on challenging peaks, usually undertaken with multiday mountaineering expeditions, such as Alaska's Denali (round trip 11 hours, 48 minutes), Mont Blanc (round trip 4 hours, 57 minutes, from Chamonix), and the Matterhorn (round trip 2 hours, 52 minutes). As part of his "Summits of My Life" project, Kilian plans to complete a speed trip up and down Mt. Everest.

I spent January, February, and March hoping Kilian wouldn't show up to run Zion before I did; I'm good at this stuff, but, like any other ultradistance runner on the planet, I'd be hard-pressed to best a mark set by Kilian. I checked the FKT website (http://fastestknowntime. proboards.com/) incessantly, hoping that he hadn't, say, read a Catalonian translation of Edward Abbey, or chanced upon a map of Utah.

When April rolled around and Kilian still hadn't posted, I headed to the desert with my support crew. This was hardly the crack crew of seasoned adventure racers or veteran competitors like my dad, as I'd had in the past. But in my new career as a solo runner, these two guys proved to be the perfect companions: my neighbor Charles Martelli and his brother-in-law, Nick Yaskoff.

Rolling through Springdale, Utah, a town of approximately 547 hardy souls at the gateway to Zion, I shared my goal with one particularly grizzled fellow we met on the road next to an emu farm as we took in the desert view.

"So, you're going to try to get across the park in less than eight hours? On foot?" he grumbled, looking up from his well-traveled mountain bike.

"Well, I actually hope to break 7:48," I mustered.

"And how many times have you been here before?"

"Umm . . . this is the first time."

Mr. Grizzled simply huffed and turned away, which I'm pretty sure was his way of telling me nicely that he thought I was in way above my head.

Although of course he didn't know that I was a professional endurance athlete, the conversation replayed in my head as I tried to fall asleep the night before the run; yet another negative story had been etched in the back of my mind.

Charles and Nick would meet me at two points along the way to supply new fuel and water bottles, and I can't stress enough their importance in the endeavor. We arrived at Lee Pass on the west side of the park at about 7:00 a.m. on April 6, and I headed out a few minutes later, without fanfare. No shotgun blast, no "Eye of the Tiger," no Le Mans start, no applause, no nothing. The start was, well, just pushing a button on my watch and waving to two buddies as I headed down a trail. "All right," I said. "See you in a while."

They waved back. "Have a good one," said Charles.

This was my welcome to the glamorous world of the solo racer.

As I cruised down the La Verkin Creek Trail at dawn, dipping in and out of the drainage surrounded by high desert brush, visions of the mountain lions who hunt in the area danced in my head, and I kept myself busy calling out, "Hey, cougar," in a weak attempt to scare them off as I came around blind corners. (I know mountain lion attacks are extremely rare, and I run alone almost every day in an area where plenty of them live, but an unfamiliar environment often gets us thinking about things that can go wrong.) Thankfully, energy-sucking sand on the trail decreased my enthusiasm enough that the catcalls stopped before I encountered my first of ten or so through-hikers as I headed northeast up La Verkin Creek itself. Flying around a corner as I cruised along the serpentine track through thick shrubs, I almost ran headfirst into the first of three backpackers coming my way, no doubt finishing their weeklong journey along the route. Excited to be almost finished and intrigued by my appearance (small pack, carrying very little, yet out in the middle of nowhere), the guy called out enthusiastically, "Hey man! What are you up to?" I chat with strangers on the trail all the time when I'm training, but all I could muster here was, "Have a good one, guys!" as I crashed through the bushes alongside the trail to rush past the stunned hikers.

I turned right and southeast off La Verkin Creek onto the Hop Valley Trail, and here encountered the first significant climb of the route. Rangers had warned that this section, and others, might be covered with deep snow and/or mud, and I was very happy to find that the trail was almost completely dry. As it turned out, the running conditions were almost ideal over the whole route. There was, of course, plenty of sand and technical terrain, as well as about 10,000 feet of both climbing and descending. All of this is unavoidable in Zion. But temperatures ranged from the mid-40s to the high 80s. For the purposes of my run, that was great.

My first time check for the run was at 13 miles, where the Hop Valley Trail crosses Kolob Terrace Road. Luke Nelson, the current record holder, had posted his 2012 splits for the run, which he did in the east to west direction (I was doing the same route, but in the opposite direction), and I had calculated his time for three segments across the route. Because ultrarunners generally slow down a bit as the run goes on, I figured I had to exceed his time on the early sections. I was a couple of minutes off my goal at the Hop Valley Trailhead, and I worked hard on the Connector Trail, heading east to its junction with the Wildcat Trail, where I would meet the crew at 16.8 miles. The Connector Trail rolls nicely through open fields and old pine forests, and I almost felt like I was at home in the Colorado Front Range.

I was enthused to hit the crew point at 2 hours, 27 minutes, and so was the crew—they had arrived just moments before! Crewing is always an adventure and a challenge, and anyone who gives up their own time to support someone else's goals has my utmost respect. Running down the trail as we fumbled bottles and dropped layers of clothing, Charles and Nick gave me a nice boost. I grabbed two bottles of Vitargo and one bottle of water. As it turned out, my entire consumption for the run was four bottles of water and four bottles of my carb drink, each with 700 calories, plus some salt pills.

I hadn't seen anyone in about 10 miles and would not for another 12—perfect! This solo run across Zion was unlike any race I'd ever done. No start or finish line, no other competitors, a small support crew. It was just me and the vastness of the national park; or, as Abbey put it, "the space and light and clarity and special strangeness of the American West."

Wildcat Canyon was a case in point, presenting a combination of forested terrain and awe-inspiring views. The climb was consistent, but not too steep, and I continued to roll, reminding myself that working hard now would get me to the finish faster. At one point on a technical descent, a scenario played out in my head in which I imagined a crash and then analyzed the likelihood of removing myself from that location with a broken ankle. Traversing technical, rocky terrain, steep slopes, and a few exposed drops, I made sure to focus on *what* I was doing—foot placement, handholds, trail junctions, safety first—in order to avoid an accident while running alone deep in the desert backcountry.

I was energized when I turned south on the West Rim Trail from the high point of the route at about 7,500 feet. I had covered 21.5 miles. Thus began my fastest segment of the journey, and I was happy to run at a pace of just over 7 minutes per mile as the trail gradually descended along the plateau overlooking white and red sandstone spires and canyons and the low desert beyond them.

Thirty one miles into my run, I passed the second Telephone Canyon Junction on the left and began descending steeply toward the Grotto (the most popular part of Zion, complete with a paved road and many tourists). My final 17 or so miles would include a steep descent of more than 2,300 feet on rocks and pavement before a climb of the same amount of elevation out of the other side of the canyon during the hottest part of the day. I was reminded of how my CU coach Mark Wetmore had described a particularly hot, windy, exposed segment of one of our regular runs in Boulder. He called it "the anvil of God."

Had the TV cameras been rolling—and of course, they rarely roll during ultradistance races of any kind, much less a solo FKT attempt—the commentators would have surely built up the idea that this final stretch, where I may or may not have the remaining energy to complete the most challenging section at the end of the route, would be the final factor in determining whether I'd chosen my direction wisely for this new stage of my life.

Thankfully, as in most ultras, the cameras weren't rolling. Unlike in most ultras, I was the only one who was tracking my location and splits—and probably the only one who cared, at least at the moment. The solitude of the journey and the vastness of the place, however, generated a deep significance for me, probably more so than anything I would have felt in an organized race. I ran hard, deeply committed to hammering to the finish.

Descending to my next crew point would involve dropping down to a stretch of 21 sharp switchbacks on a steep, paved trail that runs from the popular and accessible viewpoint near Angel's Landing,

I had to dig deep on this unforgiving descent in Zion. CREDIT: TRAVIS MACY

where I was now located, to a bus stop, campground, and ranger station on the well-used road along the North Fork Virgin River below. I let it rip on the descent, calling ahead to throngs of people making a daylong journey of the trail segment I would run down with reckless abandon in just a few minutes. "On your left," I shouted, "Pardon me." Startled hikers abruptly shifted to the right, their backpacks rustling, as I came rushing by. Some of them seemed as surprised as if I had been riding a unicycle.

Running downhill tends to trash the legs, and my body began to complain a bit. I passed the Grotto picnic area, near Zion Lodge, at mile 36. My elapsed time was 5 hours, 16 minutes, at this point, and I had about 12 miles to go. Given the upcoming climb, the technical trails, and the rising heat, covering the distance in less than 2.5 hours could not be assumed.

Ascending the East Rim Trail was the next challenge, and I would now climb more than 2,000 feet in just a few miles. The sun beat down without a cloud or tree for shade in sight. I took on some fuel, guzzled more water, and reiterated positive stories in my mind:

You can do this, Trav. The harder it gets, the stronger you are.

I had recently started coaching Charles, my support crew member, in his training for his first ultra. He had heard me talking about this venture for months, and was eager to get a taste of the route out in Zion, so I had invited him to join me on the final 12 miles to the finish. Although Charles is a great guy and his company was a nice shift, I must admit that I was deep in the racing zone and beginning to suffer a bit by that point, so I was probably not the best company. In truth, I hardly spoke a word.

Meanwhile, we were reminded that although it is relatively inaccessible, Zion is popular (there were about 2.8 million visitors in 2013). There was a constant stream of day-hikers along this stretch, and unlike some of the others we had encountered, these folks weren't startled; they were supportive, and spurred us on. As we were starting to cook in the midday sun, Charles reached out for help from a particularly well-supplied hiker, whose side pouches bulged with water bottles.

"Got any extra water for this guy?" Charles asked as he ran ahead, "He's running the entire park today!"

"The entire park? Hell, yeah!"

The guy doused me with a full water bottle as I trudged past up the hill, making me refreshed and revitalized for the homestretch through the desert.

Back on the plateau and alone again, we simply trudged on. What does one contemplate at times like these? I pondered more of Abbey's insights in *Desert Solitude*. "I became aware . . . of the immense silence in which I am lost," he wrote during one of his solo sojourns through Moab. "Not so much silence as a great stillness . . . a suspension of time, a continuous present."

I followed the narrow trail seen here on the opposite side of the river as I ascended out of the Grotto near the end of my Zion run. It was a long, hot climb! CREDIT: TRAVIS MACY

In my case, though, time was progressing, perhaps all too fast, if I hoped to set this record. I considered my stories. One of the narratives involved me staggering to a halt, cramped up or bonking; taken down by a course too long, hilly, and hot for a 30-year-old high-school teacher and father of two kids in diapers. The other narrative grew louder with each step: this was essentially the story I'm telling you now, about how I had set this goal as a way to launch a new direction in my life as an endurance athlete. It was me, in the wilderness I loved, alone and racing against the clock. I may not have had a team jersey on, and there may not have been a nattily attired race official waiting to hand me a check at the finish line as there had been during the adventure races, but I was still a top athlete, and I would still be strong

Even though there was no crowd, music, massages, or post-race expo, Charles and I were stoked to reach the finish line (marked by an old, rusty gate) in Zion. Just over a year after his ultra training started with this run, Charles, who is a working professional and father of two young children, successfully rewrote his own story and completed his first 100-miler—pretty cool! CREDIT: TRAVIS MACY

to the finish. I would break—and maybe even smash—a record that meant a great deal to me and the ultradistance community.

A few miles before the finish, I had squeezed down the pace and separated myself from Charles, who was running hard but did not have as much experience or training as me. Nick, who had hiked in from the car at the finish to meet us for the final stretch, appeared around a corner: "Come on guys, hammer it in!" The echo off the cliffs reenergized us, and we both picked up the pace.

Thinking of my family, I crossed the finish in 7 hours, 27 minutes, alongside two friends. No bands were playing, and no TV cameras or reporters awaited, but I had broken the Zion traverse record by over 20 minutes! Mission accomplished.

Records are set to be broken, and given the popularity of such FKTs, I knew my mark would not last long. Less than two months later, in fact,

GPS watches and route-sharing websites like Strava.com allow runners to document and share their FKT runs. On my Zion route, you can see that the park is laced with canyons, plateaus, and other neat features. CREDIT: TRAVIS MACY

two accomplished runners, Mike Foote and Justin Yates, ran the opposite direction across the park and bested my time by about 5 minutes. They now held the "Trans-Zion Overall Record," while I maintained the "West to East Trans-Zion Record." Such technicalities didn't really matter, though, and I expect the record for running west to east will be broken at some point anyway. What did matter, though, is that I had a new story (the good one) that *would* last and *could not* be broken by anyone else.

Ultra Mindset 7: Bad Stories, Good Stories: The Ones You Tell Yourself Make All the Difference

IN MOVIE PRODUCTION, A SOUND-ONLY RECORDING OF ONSITE background noise or narration to be used in post-production audio editing is often made, and it's called the "wild track." Think about the revolving internal monologues in many of Martin Scorsese's films, such as *The Wolf of Wall Street*, where Leonardo DiCaprio's wild track of customer-scamming, drug-fueled antics is . . . well, really wild.

Your mind also plays a wild track, and it consists of the stories that impact how you feel, what you can or can't do, and even what you believe. Some stories in the wild track boom loud and often, and others show up as leitmotifs that pipe up, almost subconsciously, from time to time or under certain conditions. I think of my wild track as the voices and self-talk that are constantly going on in my mind, both consciously and subconsciously.

The wild track matters—and probably more than you think. Negative stories often play in the wild track, reflecting our underlying anxieties and fears. Rewriting them could make a monumental difference in your outlook, potential for greatness, and overall happiness. Think about how hard you are on yourself sometimes and how that wears you down. Think about how you'd feel if, instead of weighing yourself down with self-doubt and criticism, you could reinvigorate yourself with confidence and affirmation.

Here are some of the negative stories that have run through my head over the years (many, of them, I suspect, are similar to those of a lot of young males):

1988: Man, those kids on the soccer field are good. I can't compete at that level.

1990: Savannah, that cute first grader, didn't chase me at recess. Girls don't like me.

1993: I have to go to school, play soccer, play baseball, play basketball, and hang out with my friends. I like doing all of these things, but I can't find the time to do them all as well as I want to. Lack of time is making me angry.

1994: Savannah, the cute fifth grader, dumped me right in the middle of the end-of-the-year dance. Girls don't like me.

1998: Those guys are running some fast track times. I can't compete at that level.

2000: I have to earn straight As, get into a good college, be the student body president, letter in four sports, be an All-State athlete, and hang out with my friends. I like doing all of these things, but I can't find the time to do them all as well as I want to. Lack of time is making me angry.

2000: Girls don't like me because they think I'm a school geek.

2001: I'm about to give a graduation speech for thousands of people. How can I possibly make it through this?

2001: Most of the college runners are a lot more talented than me. I can't compete at that level.

2002: I have to be a varsity athlete at CU, hold a job, earn good grades, prepare a super and diverse background that will make me attractive to medical schools, party with the cool kids, take time to visit my family, and save the world as a philanthropist hippie Boulderite. I like doing all of these things, but I can't find the time to do them all as well as I want to. Lack of time is making me angry.

2003: I'm about to do my first triathlon and I can barely swim. I might die.

2003: Girls don't like me. Period.

2004: Amy and I are getting serious. Am I really ready? Am I worthy to be this beautiful, talented young lady's boyfriend . . . and, gulp . . . possibly, husband?

2005: I just graduated from college and I'm about to race against the best and most experienced adventure racers in the world at a big race in Sweden. I can't compete at that level.

2006: I just completely crushed my collarbone in a middle-of-the-night mountain-biking crash in Moab. The season is over.

2007: I'm about to race for a week in Scotland at the Adventure Racing World Championship. Miserable, cold rain has been falling since I got here, and I know that's going to be the case for the entire, sleep-deprived journey. How can I possibly get through this?

2008: I'm a new teacher, and the "simple" task of managing the classroom is proving nearly impossible. Planning each lesson takes almost forever, and I can't seem to forecast my work and the students' progress more than a day or two in advance. It's overwhelming. Lack of time is making me angry.

2009: The economic downturn is killing sponsorship prospects. I'll never race internationally again.

2011: We've been traveling in Europe for a week with Wyatt, who's six months old. Everything is off-kilter and I'm totally sleep deprived going into a monster mountain-biking race against the best pros around that involves ascending more than 18,000 feet in the Alps around Mont Blanc and riding for eight hours or more. The promoters say it's "The Hardest Race in the World." I've done a bunch of other races that have been similarly promoted . . . but this one really might be it! I can't compete at this level.

2012: I'm going to be turning 30, I'm about to have my second child, and adventure racing isn't feasible for me anymore. . . . I'm done as an athlete!

Some of the incident-specific stories I faced were relatively easy to overcome with counter-stories. Others were not so easy. But as you just read in this chapter, I was able to overcome that last, very negative story—the combination of anxiety over turning 30, the pay freeze in the school district, and my reluctant disengagement with the adventure racing world—with a bold, new, positive story that involved, in large part, my plan to set the record at Zion. It worked!

Negative stories, I think, must be rewritten and fought with better ones. The negative ones can be insidious: some of them—often the ones that appear year after year in updated forms—have morphed into things we actually *believe* about ourselves.

So we must look them in the eye, size them up, and recognize them for exactly what they are: stories. Nothing more, nothing less. It sounds simple, and it is. But, it sure as heck isn't easy, particularly when we are chipping away at stories that have become beliefs. Personally, I find the following steps to be helpful in battling negative stories. This is just what I did when I needed to create a new story in 2013 and came up with my Zion solo run:

1. Sit down and write out the negative story.
   ▸ *I've got two kids and I'm 30 years old. It's going to be impossible to continue racing at a high level.*

2. Read it and reread it. Recognize it for what it is: just a few words . . . just a story . . . nothing that should have the power to rule you.
   ▸ *This is one option for what I can believe. Many people might believe they can't pursue goals alongside parenting and working, but I think it's just a story. I don't have to believe it if I don't want to.*

3. Write out positive alternatives that can be used to battle it, and find your new "plot" for a positive story. Could it be a new goal? Changing a behavior? Eliminating the negative?
   ▸ *I may be busy if I parent, work, and compete, but I'll be a better parent and professional if I take time to release anxiety and energy by training. Focus on a single sport will take less time than adventure racing, and I'm pretty sure I can still be competitive. By focusing only on running for the first time since college, I can address relative weaknesses and get better—cool! I'll set a goal to ensure the hard work happens, culminating in a definable endpoint.*

4. Turn one or more of these positive alternatives into a mantra. Write it, say it, post it where you'll see it. Be sure to say it, either in your head or out loud, when the negative story comes calling. Say it a lot during mental training activities, like a nice, long run or a walk, when it's cold and dark and lonely.
   ▸ *"Make the most of your life, Trav."*

5. Determine what you will do to prove that the negative story is not true and the positive story is true. This is maybe the most important step.

> ▸ *I'll go run across Zion National Park, perhaps faster than any-*
> *one has ever done it.*

6. Actually, this is the most important step: repeat the actions
   above, in any order, as many times as they need to be repeated.
   If necessary, for years and years.

   > ▸*Maybe I can back that up by winning the Leadman series later*
   > *in the summer.*

The power of transformational self-storytelling has been studied
and written about. In his 2001 book *The Woo Way: A New Way of Living
and Being*, Jim Downton Jr., a sociology professor at CU, examines the
power of negative stories—and also the power of acting and thinking
intentionally to change the script.

Shawn Achor is a psychologist and teacher at Harvard University
and CEO of Good Think, Inc., where he teaches about and researches
positive psychology. In his TED talk "The Happy Secret to Better
Work," Achor notes, "The lens through which your brain views the
world changes your reality. Seventy-five percent of job successes are
predicted by your optimism levels, your social support, and your ability to see stress as a challenge instead of a threat." In other words, stories do matter, and you should tell yourself positive ones. Achor goes
on to argue that, although we often tell ourselves that the next success
will finally lead to happiness, happiness generally *precedes* success. I've
tried it both ways, and I agree with Achor.

In his creative and inspirational text *The Icarus Deception*, Seth
Godin presents more ideas related to overcoming negative stories.
If you are battling a problem, he says, one simple way to whittle it
down to something manageable is to get an index card and write
"Problem" on one side and "Solution" on the other. Write, in one
short sentence, the problem in its space. Then, give the card to some-
one else and have them write a simple solution on the other side.
Your problem may or may not be solved, but it should at least be

diminished and clarified, and you may have gained a valuable new perspective. I like that.

In some cases, says Godin, you might also realize that the problem that is dragging you down with negative stories is, in fact, completely irrelevant, because it cannot be solved. Discovering that your problem can't be solved can often be a cause for relief, because an issue that is beyond your control is an issue that you really shouldn't worry about. As psychologists would say, it's outside of your "locus of control," so there's no point in stressing over it. Obviously, there are exceptions to that, but by and large, the idea of worrying about only what we *can* do something about is, I believe, a sound approach to life.

Even in a dire situation, recognizing that it's something beyond control or a dilemma to which there is no answer can allow you to move on and take the next step, thus giving you the ability to shift your focus to what you *can* do. For example, maybe you can get through the situation with dignity and grace. Or you can offer support and inspiration to someone else facing the same problem. Or dedicate your energies to the cause or for a cure (a good example here from the running world would be the many participants in the Leukemia Society's "Team in Training" program who have decided to raise money and complete a marathon in memory of a loved one afflicted by the disease).

Remember: Even if they can't be solved, problems can usually be opportunities to learn and grow. As Dr. Steven Jonas says, "there are no bad experiences."

Sometimes, we come to a point at which one of our "new" stories has become outdated or less than optimal. Such was the case for me with the paragraph below:

Here's an example of a negative story in my life that I recognize is unsolv-able: ~~*While working full-time, I'm also working hard in endurance coaching, motivational speaking, and writing. How can I possibly get through this? Lack of time is making me angry.*~~

This was an improved story over an earlier one, but, as it turns out, it was not as good as I could do, and that is why I have crossed it out with a strikethrough. I stand by the point that some negative stories are unsolvable. For me, though, overwhelming busyness is no longer one of them. Reading Brené Brown's *Daring Greatly* made me realize that, for many years, I had been judging my own worth, at least in part, according to how busy I was; this is not particularly uncommon here in America. I now have a new story, one that's recommended by Brown:

I am "Cultivating Play and Rest . . . [by] Letting Go of Exhaustion as a Status Symbol and Productivity as Self-Worth."

I'm pleased to report that this new story is making me happier, more confident, and, ironically, more efficient and effective as a professional.

All new stories are not created equal, and exactly how we go about rewriting our stories deserves some attention. Take a look at the stories a competitive athlete might tell him or herself:

A) I can't compete at that level.

B) I can compete at that level, and I'm going to win easily because I'm good! Yeah!

C) I can compete at that level, and it's going to take a lot of hard work, including overcoming challenges X, Y, and Z, which will not be easy and will probably be painful at times.

We've all told ourselves Story A, and we know from the discussion above that it really is just a story. Story B is an interesting case. It's positive and empowering, and it directly contradicts the harmful, negative predecessor. It's a type of story that confident optimists like me often fall into. Story C, as you may have seen very quickly, is probably the best option. Heidi Grant Halvorson, PhD, in *Succeed: How We Can*

Reach Our Goals, talks about "mental contrasting," which is basically a process that involves intentionally juxtaposing the positive outcomes associated with meeting a goal with the challenges that are inherently involved in completing any worthwhile endeavor. Science shows, according to Halvorson, that including details about the challenges to be faced as essential elements of the stories we tell ourselves is crucial in identifying the work that will be done to achieve a goal—and in motivating ourselves to do that work.

Mindset 7 REFLECTION

It's time to dial in to your wild track, rewrite at least one negative story, and think about the better one that you can use to replace it.

1. Sit down and write out the negative story.

_____

_____

_____

_____

_____

2. Read it and reread it. Recognize it for what it is: just a few words . . . just a story . . . nothing that should have the power to rule you. What have you learned?

_____

_____

_____

_____

_____

3. Write out positive alternatives that can be used to battle it, and find your new "plot" for a positive story. Could it be a new goal? Changing a behavior? Eliminating the negative?

_____

_____

_____

_____

_____

4. Turn one or more of these positive alternatives into a mantra. Write it, say it, post it where you'll see it. Be sure to say it, either in your head or out loud, when the negative story comes calling. Say it a lot during mental training activities, like a nice, long run or a walk, when it's cold and dark and lonely. What's your mantra?

_____

_____

_____

_____

_____

5. Determine what you will do to prove that the negative story is not true and the positive story is true. This is maybe the most important step.

_____

_____

_____

_____

_____

6. Actually, this is the most important step: repeat the actions above, in any order, as many times as they need to be repeated. If necessary, for years and years. How and when will you reinforce your new story?

_____

_____

_____

_____

_____

Mindset 7 ACTIVITY: The Hour of Power: Tempo Run + Story Time

Ever been limited on time and in need of burning off some steam? Who hasn't!? This is a great workout when those two factors converge.

Mental training: The Hour of Power uses hard aerobic exercise to develop rich conditions for listening to your wild track and for a 20-minute thinking session about the stories you are telling yourself—and how to rewrite them, if needed. A frenzied daily life can make it hard for us to even hear our wild tracks. To use the terminology of master wellness and life coach Margaret Moore (aka Coach Meg) in the 2011 *Organize Your Mind, Organize Your Life*, I've learned that "taming the frenzy" of fast-paced thoughts flying through my mind throughout the day's activities by going on a hard run or ride is often the best way to quickly access the stories that play such an important role.

Physical training: Boost your aerobic conditioning with 20 minutes of hard exercise and 40 minutes of foundation work.

When: This time-efficient workout is excellent when you have just an hour to spare, such as early in the morning, late at night, or at lunchtime. The Hour of Power is handy because it can be done inside or outside and either on a bike or in running shoes. You can even do it pushing a stroller or pulling a bike trailer.

How: Run or bike 20 minutes easy as a warm up. Move directly into running or biking 20 minutes fairly hard, at a level of 3 or 4 on a scale of 1 to 5 (with 5 being an all-out pace you could hold for just a few minutes). During this hard push, you should be breathing hard enough that talking in full sentences is challenging. Cool down with another 20 minutes at an easy effort. During the cool down, when the endorphins are flowing and your thinking is clear and free of frenzied clutter, think about your stories: What's playing on your wild track? Are the stories good, bad, or neutral? Which stories need rewriting?

Extra: I often feel refreshed, as if I have been given a new outlook on life, after just 20 minutes of hard exercise like this. Try comparing the stories from your wild track before and after your hard push. Are there any differences, and what's the take-away?

Mindset 7 LEARN

Ray Zahab

RACING LIFE

Ray describes himself as "a former pack-a-day smoker who realized one day that my life needed a change." He picked up endurance sports, found ultrarunning, and soon was competing in ultras around the world, eventually running across the entire Sahara Desert in an epic, 111-day, 7,500-kilometer crossing with two other runners.

REAL LIFE

Ray has built an inspirational and educational learning platform at the i2P (www.impossible2Possible.com) website, which creates and shares "adventures that inspire and educate youth to protect this fragile planet and its people." The program is the real deal, and it blends outdoor adventure, technology, education, and youth leadership in incredible ways (see also www.rayzahab.com).

RAY'S THOUGHTS ON THE STORIES WE TELL OURSELVES

1. *Never underestimate yourself!*

   As human beings we are good at talking ourselves out of something before we take a risk. We see people at their high points of success, but they have actually had many ups and downs to get to that point. It's a long journey, and the people who succeed never underestimate themselves. The people who succeed tell themselves they can do this, and they do it!

2. *Be resilient.*

   This is a key to everything we do in life. The greater the goal, the harder it will be to achieve. Anticipate that setbacks will exist, and view them as opportunities to learn. Never give up, and keep on telling yourself stories about how resilient you are!

3. *Remain humble even when the good stories turn out to be great!*

   Never rest on your laurels, never think you have it all figured out, and always keep learning. Ask for help, and realize that it's all a process and you will always continue to grow.

—Ray

Never Quit . . . Except
When You Should Quit

THINK OF IT AS AN ULTRA DECATHLON: A RACE IN which competitors complete a 26.2-mile trail marathon, a 50-mile mountain-bike race, a 100-mile mountain-bike race, and a 100-mile trail run. Throw in a 10K running race the day after biking 100 miles (for God-knows-why), set the whole thing high in the Rockies, and you have Leadman, a sort of six-week immersion into endurance hell that I wanted to win in 2013 more than almost anything else in the world.

Leadville had been in my thoughts and dreams since I was a boy watching my dad, ill-prepared, hallucinate and hobble his way to the finish line back in 1988. Years later, when I heard about the six-week supersized version of the Leadville 100, I realized *that's* how I wanted to do it. I wanted to become not only a

Leadville finisher, but a Leadman. It takes mettle to achieve this metallic title: one becomes a Leadman by successfully completing each of the five Leadville Race Series events over the course of six weeks during the summer. It starts with a trail-running marathon that peaks high on Mosquito Pass. Two weeks later, you race on a mountain bike for 50 miles over steep, rocky terrain.

Either of those two events alone could be the capstone of a normal racing season and would be followed by weeks of recovery and less intense training. Not for a Leadman competitor. Less than a month later, over the course of eight brutal days, you mountain bike 100 miles, run a 10K road race (the day after the bike ride, adding insult to injury), and then, the following weekend, race the Leadville 100 run as the grand finale.

Each race is contested at elevations between 10,200 and 13,186 feet, each involves significant climbing and descending on rocky trails, and each presents a significant challenge of its own. Blogger and coach Richard Diaz put it well, calling Leadman an event that "makes the term 'Ultra' seem inadequate."

Who came up with this strange and torturous schedule, and why? Not surprisingly, it was the same character who had founded the Leadville 100 Run in 1983: Ken Chlouber, a man who's part Old West, part New Age. The shotgun blasts with which he starts each edition of the race are equaled in volume and intensity by the barrage of his self-empowerment calls to action—as evidenced by his explanation for what gave him the idea of expanding the 100-miler into a series of ultra-endurance tests. "We started these events in Leadville based on two principles," said Chlouber when I called him to ask about it. "The first is, 'don't quit.' That same damn principle applies to your work and your family and these brutal races and whatever else you do in life. The second is 'do more.' I've said, 'You're better than you think you are, you can do more than you think you can' one thousand times, and I mean it. Leadman is all about doing more. We wanted to give athletes a chance to push their physical and mental capabilities to the true maximum, and that's what Leadman has done. Leadman is the real deal, and if you want to make it through you're gonna have to tell yourself 'DON'T QUIT' a hell of a lot out there."

Despite Chlouber's rhetoric, only four people finished Leadman in its first year, 2003. A husband-wife pair from Santa Fe, New Mexico, named Jan and Kim Bear, whom I knew from the adventure racing scene as the "Bear Pair," were the initial victors: the first Leadman and Leadwoman (titles that, admittedly, make them sound like characters in a superhero comic book). Jan's cumulative time was 47 hours, 38 minutes, and the bar was set for the male record. No more than eight athletes finished Leadman in any year prior to 2008, and while numbers have grown a bit, just 35 athletes finished in 2012, the year before I was planning to tackle it. Most years, fewer than half of the starters complete the series. In 2012, a new event record was set by Tim Waggoner, who became the first athlete to complete the series in a cumulative time of under 40 hours. Waggoner is a competitive runner and former pro triathlete; I knew his time of 37 hours, 45 minutes, would be tough to beat.

Recovering from my Zion run in the spring of 2013, I reflected on my personal racing history in Leadville, eventually wagering that I had done enough to be well-prepared for Leadman. I had been snowshoe racing there for almost 20 years, and though most of these events lasted no more than 2 hours, the 20-miler had provided some real mental training, and even the short races had been solid pushes at altitude in extreme winter conditions. My first Leadville Race Series event was the 100-mile mountain-bike ride in 2007, where I finished twelfth in a time of 7 hours, 56 minutes. At that point, Lance Armstrong and the other top pros had not started competing at Leadville, so breaking 8 hours in the bike race was almost good enough for the top ten. Not so when I wheeled to the line again in 2011! I had become a much better mountain biker—and the race had become much more competitive. I finished in 7 hours, 15 minutes, a time that would have won the race in its early days, good enough for twenty-sixth place. The year prior, I had won Leadville's Silver Rush 50 Mountain Bike Race, setting a course record of 3 hours, 52 minutes, so falling this far back in the field was a bit of a surprise . . . and also a sign of how many very powerful mountain bikers with strong road riding ability were now doing the race (the 100 bike course has quite a bit of relatively flat road terrain).

In 2010, I also competed in the first (and, as it turned out, last) 24 Hours of Leadville Mountain Bike Race (apparently, most people don't like riding at above 10,200 feet all day and night). I rode 205 miles in 12 laps of a tough, mountainous course and won the race, besting many of the teams competing as relay riders. I guess that's one record I'll be able to hold onto for good, even if only by default. In 2012, I had finished third in the competitive Bailey Hundo, a 100-mile mountain-bike race on the Colorado Trail and other technical terrain and hilly roads around the legendary Buffalo Creek area, just south of Evergreen near Bailey, Colorado. There, I rode 100 miles in 6 hours, 44 minutes, and going into Leadman, I figured I could put some time on the competition on the bike if my fitness was anything like it had been at the Hundo.

What made the Leadman especially challenging was that this was not a typical race, where I needed to summon up my courage for one day, or, in the case of the team experiences, one week. I had to banish my fears, assert confidence and positivity, and deliver peak performances not once, not even twice, but five times over a period of six weeks. If I gained a lead through the early events, my fear could increase, because I might start to feel like it had become "my race to lose." It would be quite a test, even for the Ultra Mindset.

The first part of this endurance exam was June 29 at the Leadville Trail Marathon.

LEADMAN: EVENT 1
TRAIL RUNNING MARATHON

The marathon course gains 6,333 feet in elevation, which is kind of like running up the Empire State Building four times. The terrain includes a little bit of pavement, a few miles on dirt roads, some technical single-track with plenty of rocks hidden by overgrown bushes, and a whole lot of slippery, loose, rocky, and steep old mining roads. Imagine running down a ski slope covered with unstable river rocks, and you'll get a feel for many of the descents on this course.

Sixty-nine men and 18 women took on the Leadman quest in 2013. Though our goals and backgrounds varied, we shared the singular vision of completing five challenging, high-altitude endurance races over the next six weeks.

I knew going into it that the competition would be tight. Bob Africa, a strong ultrarunner and adventure racer from Boulder who trained periodically with his friend Scott Jurek, a legendary ultrarunner, wanted to make a fortieth birthday statement at Leadman. I had done some multisport races against Luke Jay, a 32-year-old from Littleton, Colorado, who also has a strong adventure-racing background, and I figured he would be solid. There was rock-solid Tim Long, who was being coached by Tim "Lucho" Waggoner, the guy who had who won and set a Leadman series record the previous year. At 26, Leadville's own Marco Peinado was the young gun of the series. Everyone knew he could run, and he was definitely a guy to keep an eye on.

As the first race in the series, the Leadville Trail Marathon was integral to setting a tone for the next six weeks. On race day, the gun blast early in the morning sparked a crazy surge from a few runners; the simultaneous start of our marathon with a separate half-marathon meant it was hard to tell whether or not to pay attention to particular racers. When the courses split after a mile or so, I could see that just two marathoners were ahead. One of them, the leader, was Marshall Thomson.

Since the Leadville Race Series, rather than this particular event, was my top goal, I knew I had to run my own race. Nonetheless, I didn't want Thomson, the previous year's winner, to get too far ahead. Although he was running to win this race alone, not the race series, I wanted to send a message to my competition. I figured ten minutes into the series was as good a time as any to let them know I meant business, so much so that I could keep up with Thomson, a very talented runner from Crested Butte who once survived a direct lightning strike while mountain biking.

The route climbs consistently from the start at 10,200 feet in downtown Leadville to a high point of almost 12,200 feet on Ball Mountain. There's a steep climb just before this high point—I knew it well because the Silver Rush 50 Mountain Bike Race also goes there—and I did a bit of power hiking to conserve energy. My plan was to take care of myself and hold steady for the first 16 miles before really thinking about racing, and fuel and hydration were integral to this concept (as they are in any endurance race).

I had sipped on a bottle of Vitargo for this first part of the race, and it was empty as I reached the aid station at about 10 miles, which was conveniently located at the base of a 3-mile, 2,000-foot climb to the turnaround on Mosquito Pass at 13,186 feet. The six especially steep and rocky miles up and down Mosquito were the crux of the course, and I was looking forward to grabbing a full bottle from my friend Tim, who was planning on bringing it to the aid station. Fuel in hand, I figured, I just might be able to use the steep terrain to gain some ground on Thomson, who was two or three minutes ahead of me as we rolled down a quick descent on a dirt road.

The area around the aid station was packed with half-marathon runners (their course rejoined ours for the trek up and down Mosquito

Pass), and fans were on the sidelines, ringing cowbells and clapping. I ran through the din looking for Tim and my fuel bottle. I figured he must be among the crowd along the road after the aid tables. Fifty yards later, however, as the crowd thinned out and I still hadn't seen him, fear struck.

I stopped, turned, looked around, and yelled: "TIM!"

A few onlookers turned, but none of them was Tim, and none of them offered a bottle of Vitargo, or anything else for that matter.

In racing, as in life, it's amazing how quickly the mind can shift from positive and confident to fearful and unsure, and within seconds a litany of fears stormed my brain.

How long will it take me to get back to the aid station? How much time will Thomson gain? And who will pass me? What food will be available there? And will it make me sick? Will Tim even be here when I pass through the point again in 6 miles? I'm only about 10 miles into 282.4 miles of racing this summer, and I'm already having issues.

Then a different voice in my head weighed in:

No whining.

When I was a kid, that was Dad's biggest (and, as evidenced by the frequent pasta fights my sister and I had with him at the dinner table, possibly only) rule when he watched us on evenings while Mom was away. It seemed appropriate here. I may have barged my way through a throng of back-of-the-pack half-marathoners who were patiently awaiting their turn at the aid station tables, but I'm proud to say I didn't whine as I shoved a bunch of gels in my jersey, filled up my bottle, and headed up the hill. The time had been lost, I would have to forgo my preferred drink for the generic fluids and foods offered at the aid station, and worrying wouldn't do any good.

I felt good at the top of Mosquito Pass, and seeing Dad, who was not doing the race but had run up there for fun, gave me a nice boost. I wanted to tell him how the words he had told us when we were kids had just helped to keep me from an adult meltdown. But there wasn't time. Thomson was four or five minutes ahead, and I realized, as I headed down and saw them coming up to the turnaround, that a bunch of Leadman competitors, including Marco Peinado, Luke Jay, and Bob Africa, were all close at hand. These guys had clearly trained hard, and nothing was going to come easy this summer!

Going back the other way, this time at 16 miles, I found Tim on the far side of the aid station. He apologized and described the traffic jam on the mining road earlier in the day. I told him not to worry, because now I wasn't worried. I'd banished the fear, this time by reminding myself that whining was not an option, and deciding not to worry about a delay I couldn't control.

Fleeting glances of Thomson up ahead over the return route told me I might be gaining on him, and when volunteers told me the gap was three or four minutes, with 4 miles left, I pushed down the gas for the final, steep, rocky descent to Leadville.

I was feeling good and stoked to race! "Come on, Trav. This is what you live for," added that good old voice inside.

Quick strides and a forward lean brought me furiously down the narrow, washed-out mining road. I was going just over five minutes per mile as I made the final turn onto Sixth Street in Leadville, letting it rip for all I was worth, imagining myself as a younger runner hammering it out in a CU jersey or on the track for Coach Haebe's 200-meter repeats!

Thomson crossed the line first in a 3:37:07 win. I came across in 3:38:52, happy to celebrate with Amy, Wyatt, and Lila, who were waiting at the finish line (and before you compare those times with sea-level road marathoning, consider that, of the 489 runners who finished under the cutoff time of 9 hours and 30 minutes, only 56 of them broke five hours).

The next Leadman, and third overall, was Marco Peinado, about 20 minutes back, and Africa and Jay followed shortly. Clearly, pressing hard in this race had made a difference. I had sent the message I

I didn't win the marathon, but I couldn't help but smile when I saw Amy, Wyatt (foreground), and Lila waiting for me at the finish. This is still one of my favorite pictures, and, to me, it supports the idea that having kids is a reason to follow your own dreams. CREDIT: MACY FAMILY

needed to. Now, for a change, maybe those guys could worry about me for the next two weeks.

LEADMAN: EVENT 2
50-MILE SILVER RUSH MOUNTAIN BIKE RACE

If I had any notion of easing into the first bike race of the Leadman series, the Silver Rush 50 course eliminated that possibility altogether. The first 100 yards of the course head straight up a rocky, treeless field. There's no road or trail. Actual riding is impossible, and racers can either push or carry their bikes. The real killer is that this expanse immediately funnels into a single track at the top of the hill, so if you want to get in a good position for the race, you should probably run pretty hard up that hill. The race organization adds further enticement to those aiming to be in the lead by awarding silver coins to the first man and first woman up the hill.

The steep, hike-a-bike start at the Silver Rush 50 is always a baptism by fire. I usually run the hill fairly hard to make sure I'm near the front when the course funnels into a single track just a few minutes later. CREDIT: MACY FAMILY

In 2010, I'd won this race and set what was then the course record. That always gives one a little bit of extra incentive and confidence the next time around. And, as I would find out just a few minutes after running up that steep hill with my bike on my back, maybe even a bit of hubris.

The lung-busting run put me in good position, and I was leading the race after passing one guy just after the end of the short single-track. Back on our bikes, we turned on to one of the many old, double-track mining roads that crisscross the Leadville landscape, and I was just where I wanted to be—right up front. Things were shaping up well, and I felt strong. In 2010, I had looked back after about five minutes to see that just a few guys were with me, and I expected to see the same as I rotated for a glance.

Fear struck immediately as I discovered a long line of riders, all cruising comfortably in my draft. The pace jumped a notch when one of the guys behind me surged, pulling other guys through with him. And it skyrocketed to the "oh shit" level moments later, when another guy's hard acceleration splintered the big group, signaling that the racing was really on—and leaving me in the dust. An explosive surge ahead by fresh riders who have been drafting is the lead rider's worst nightmare, because he's been working the hardest most recently to pull the train. I was that poor guy at this moment, and, unable to match the quick accelerations, I was quickly in no-man's-land—never a good place in a bike race—about 15 places from the front and without a wheel to draft off for recovery.

I feared losing Leadman then and there, and dealing with this fear would be the story of the race.

Going into severe oxygen debt, as I had just done, does some funny things to your body. You can feel your pulse in your neck, just below the jaw on both sides. You can get a headache and begin to feel dizzy. Power output can begin to drop, and, sometimes, your thoughts become hazy. Such was the case for me, and the high altitude aggravated all of the above.

Stig Somme, a 42-year-old surgeon from Denver with whom I train periodically, cruised by me, looking strong. When he told me to tuck in and ride along in his slipstream, all I could muster was a grunt before he pulled away.

A brief descent after the first long climb provided a bit of recovery, and I seemed to at least be holding a position around tenth as we climbed sharply to above 12,000 feet at around 20 miles. Looking ahead, I could see a couple of riders using the high gearing reserved for tired legs on the steepest of climbs. "Come on, baby," uttered that inner voice. "They're suffering more than you." It became a mantra, repeated in unison with my pedal strokes.

Then another voice, not so positive:

There might be a Leadman or two ahead, and I'm not feeling good.

The battle of inner stories was on, and I finally began to overcome the fear around mile 27, ascending the steepest hill of the course. I had ridden 95 percent of this hill in 2010, but in 2013 this was not even a possibility. Interestingly, though, as soon as I hopped (well, tipped) off my bike and began to power-hike, rolling my bike alongside me, I found myself gaining on the two guys in sight ahead. I had been running much more than I did in 2010, and I was in great shape for steep hiking with the bike; my confidence grew as I passed these competitors and hopped back on at a high mountain pass.

The higher we go, the stronger we get.

The new mantra was a good one, and it kept me cruising on each climb over the second half of the race. My whole family was at the race, and the fuel and hydration I grabbed from them at the turnaround were kicking in.

I hung on to the "getting stronger" story as a means of mitigating my Leadman fears, and my performance improved as my outlook became more positive. The two played off each other. (This performance/outlook parallel generally proves true for me in life in general as well; the better I feel, the better I'm doing. How about you?)

The final descent to the Silver Rush 50 finish line was fast and furious, and I thought I was cranking along until a competitor flew by me as if I were riding Wyatt's bike with the training wheels. Chasing furiously, I blew through a turn and rode about a minute off course before turning around. Fear struck again, and I hammered to the finish, unsure of my place among the Leadmen.

I had finished ninth overall and first among Leadmen, it turns out, and my time of 4:07 enabled me to hang on to the top spot. At this point, we had raced 76 miles, but 206 more remained. The Leadville 100 Mountain Bike Race was four weeks away.

I didn't have my best day at the Silver Rush 50 bike race, but I couldn't help but smile when I crossed the finish line to find Wyatt riding an ATV with, who else, Leadville 100 founder Ken Chlouber himself. Chlouber has always talked about the "Leadville family," and even since the integration of corporate sponsorship from Lifetime Fitness, the family spirit persists. CREDIT: TRAVIS MACY

I thought I would have a month to prepare myself mentally and physically for the final Leadman push. But then life intervened, and I had to practice my fear-management skills and decide whether to quit or not in an entirely different arena.

My Principal Fear

Earlier in the year, I had applied for and enrolled in a graduate program through CU-Boulder that would certify me as a school principal. I had been a strong leader in the schools in which I taught, and it seemed that everyone—my colleagues, my friends, my parents, my wife—thought I should work toward becoming principal of my alma mater, Evergreen High School. Predictions of my guaranteed success in this job came from every corner: I'd do a great job there; I'd be a leader in the community; I'd influence students' lives; I'd know how to deal with parents; and—this one from inside my own head—I'd make significantly more money than I did as a teacher.

There was only one person doubting Mr. Macy's quest to become a public-school principal, and his name was Travis Macy. Was I thoroughly convinced that I would be greatly fulfilled with work in this role? No. Did I honestly think the demands of being a principal at a high school would still allow me the same time to train and be with my growing family? No. Did I think I would enjoy the work more than teaching? No.

Why, then, did I even think about it?

Fear. That's why.

For almost a decade, my income—or lack thereof—from teaching had generated fear. I was facing short-term pressure to afford the mortgage and preschool tuition in a community where the cost of living had risen significantly, combined with long-term insecurity over the thought that when the time came, we wouldn't be able to afford college tuition for two kids and retirement for two adults. That's what motivated me to enter the degree program. Fear. And that's what I was battling a few weeks before the 100-mile bike ride. Discussions with Amy and my parents helped, but I knew I had to solve this on my own.

About a week before the 100-mile bike race, I left after dinner and drove an hour west from my house to Mt. Evans. I needed to follow the lead of Edward Abbey, and retreat to the solitude of the outdoors, in order to ponder this big question in my life. I could see the lights of Evergreen, where my wife and kids were sleeping, down the valley to the east . . . and somewhere to the west in the dark, empty mountains lay Leadville. I was in between these two important spots, and I knew I was also at a crossroads in life. I had come here to camp alone in the back of my truck, away from all but my wild track, the bright, endless stars, and my big question:

Should I quit the principal licensure program and pursue a different course?

And if I was going to commit to the program, was I doing so because of a genuine desire to stay the course—or was I being driven by fear?

I thought about what I wanted out of life. I thought about my wife and my kids and how to best support them. I thought about Dad and all he had taught me. Most of all, I thought about Mom and how, under the most pressing circumstances, she had refused to live a life governed by fear.

Neither Dad nor I is half as tough as Mom, who has never run an ultra in her life. When Mom and Dad got married in 1977, a blood test revealed that she had a serious liver disease. Five years later, my parents knew a pregnancy might carry some risk, but they chose optimism, and everything went just fine for my gestation and birth. A few years after that, when I was seven, my mom got really sick, and the doctors told her she would need a liver transplant to survive. I know now that it was a matter of life and death, and the stress must have been significant for my parents, who had to consider me and my sister, Katelyn (adopted when I was two), in every decision.

But what I knew then was that when we visited Mom in the hospital after the transplant, all she wanted to talk about was how we were doing in school, and whether Uncle Brian, who was staying with us while she was in the hospital, had cooked us his famous fish sticks and French fries (he had), and whether we liked it when he cut our hair at the "barber shop" he had set up on the front porch (we did), and whether we knew how much Uncle Brian, Aunt Jan, and Uncle Eric (her other siblings were also helping out) loved us (we did). We pushed her in her wheelchair up and down the hospital corridors, and she—knowing that she might not survive to see us as teenagers—smiled and laughed and made us feel safe, as if she didn't have a care in the world, and so neither should we.

Ten years later, after adopting another baby, my sister Dona, and serving as a foster mother for two other children, Mom found out she had hepatitis C, which she had obtained from a blood transfusion she had received during her transplant. From 2000 to 2002, during my final year of high school and first years of college, she fought the disease through a relentless drive and an equally aggressive medicine protocol. The meds finally mitigated hepatitis, but they, along with the disease itself and her ongoing immunosuppressant drugs for the liver transplant, had ruined her kidneys. So in 2002, Mom received a new kidney—from her brother, Uncle Brian, fish-stick cooker, barber, and, not so incidentally, ultrarunner and mountain biker.

I know now what I didn't know then—how frightened she was. But when she was going through all the illness and the operations and the recovery, she didn't act scared. She woke up every day, she loved her family, she drove us around to soccer and cooked and put us to bed and pushed us and loved us, she did what she could do (which was still far more than most parents), and she loved us some more. Today—even though she still has to take immunosuppressants, which have led to chronic difficulties with infection and even some more surgeries—I don't know of a more loving wife, mother, or grand-mother. She has shown more toughness than I have ever witnessed in any desert or on any mountain.

I thought about my mom as I sat near the top of Mt. Evans, gazing up at the endless stars. I thought about her, about me, and about my fears.

Fear is natural. Fear of failure, of injury, of sickness and death. But people—like Mom—who have to confront life-and-death challenges on a daily basis, not because they're choosing to test themselves, but because it's just the way things are—provide the most powerful exam-ples I know of for how to deal with any fear.

While Dad and I, and most of the ultrarunners and adventure racers we know, have taken on suffering by choice, many people are forced to face suffering head-on, without choice, without options. You may be one of these people, and you probably know some others. Mom is one of these people, and her positive attitude, unwavering commitment, incredible ability to never whine, and, most significantly, ability to carry out a life that is not ruled by fear make her, hands down, the true master of the Ultra Mindset in our family.

Inspired by Mom's journey, and in a reflective mood up there at night on the mountain, I began to write:

It's 10:10 p.m., and I'm in my truck at 12,800 feet next to Summit Lake on Mt. Evans in the Colorado Rockies. Yes, the stars here are just incredible.

With two races down and three to go, I'm leading the Leadman. Racing Leadman has been a lifetime in the making for me, and committing to it and carrying out the necessary training has come fairly smoothly to me. Other things don't, however, and I'm here most importantly to offer my commitment to you. I've never run 100 miles, but that will be my task on August 17, and I know I will make it because I have committed to it. That's easy for me to say, and doing it will be fairly straightforward, in a crooked sort of way. Simply put, the choice to quit has been categorically removed as an option, so all I have to do is keep on going until I finish.

I made another choice today: I have decided to quit the principal licensure program. I'll lose the money I paid and time I invested, but I'll be able to move in a more meaningful direction.

And I'm making a commitment: I'm going to write a book that can help people reach their goals, and maybe change their lives for the better. I have wanted to write this book for a long time, but fear prevented me from making this commitment. I know it will be an uphill battle, but I'm glad my fear is gone, and I'm glad committing has removed the choice to quit.

Nothing is guaranteed, and my commitment scares the shit out of me. Simply by committing and removing the option of not reaching the finish line, I know I will make it there, and I believe that this will be true for anything one wholeheartedly commits to.

I slept well that night, and over the course of the next ten nights leading up to Leadman.

LEADMAN: EVENT 3
LEADVILLE 100 MOUNTAIN BIKE RACE

Like most endurance events, the Leadville 100 bike race starts early in the morning, 6:00 a.m., to be exact. This is good because it means less riding in the evening. Anywhere over 10,000 feet, it also means that racers are shivering on the starting line—and in this race there's no chance of warming up soon because the first few miles are downhill on pavement. And with 2,000 other people in the race, you know you're going to be riding in a huge, fast, dangerous pack over those initial miles, which are led out by a pace car that prevents anyone from breaking away and keeps the group together. Although the Tour de France riders make it look easy, road riding in a peloton at high speed on curvy mountain roads actually takes a lot of practice. Unless you do it regularly, like they do, it's nerve-wracking. There's at least one serious crash every year in the first few minutes of Leadville, and my goal every year is to simply ride at the outside edge of the sea of bodies, bikes, and testosterone in an effort to stay safe. Give me a rocky, technical trail, and I'll bomb down it, letting experience, gravity, and my bike's suspension do the work. Put me in the peloton, and I'll put on a good face: a face that's masking fear.

I escaped the crashes early on, but I was a couple hundred places back going into the first climb on the trails. Known to riders as St. Kevin's, this steep pitch that rises about 1,900 feet over 4 miles and quickly tests riders' altitude acclimatization and general readiness. The top racers go all out on it, typically breaking apart the main pack and establishing a group of up to ten or so athletes who will battle it out for the win. Leadville may be a long race, but if you want to win it, you better have a high-end speed that's out of this world.

As with the earlier marathon, my goal in the 100-mile bike race was not to finish first, but to put more time between myself and the Leadman competitors.

Heading up St. Kevin's, I was glad to see that I could climb faster than the people around me and with apparently less effort. We runners and riders generally listen and look as we pass (or get passed): How hard is he breathing? Harder than me? What's his cadence? Is he standing or sitting? Is he walking or running? How does his body look? His face? The whites of his eyes? Are they bloodshot? Thousands of data points, taken in subconsciously throughout the race, tell us how we are doing compared to those around us. As I would find out a week later, these signals can do a lot to make or break an athlete's Ultra Mindset.

I had gone out easy, and the people I was riding with had, for the most part, gone out hard. Descending dirt and pavement on the back of St. Kevin's, I found myself in a big bunch that included Leadman Bob Africa, who was surrounded by at least five of his cycling teammates. Leadville is a solo rather than a team race, but drafting tactics still play a big role. Teammates (defined here as riders who share the same sponsor and wear the same racing kits) are likely to pull for each other and help out. I was sitting just behind and to the side of Bob, and it was readily apparent to me that his vitals were steady; he was cruising along comfortably among teammates on the gradual road climb leading to Sugarloaf, the next rise, which would take us up yet another 1,000 feet. Bob had been getting stronger all summer, and now he was right with me. More fear for me.

Yet, I responded with a strong surge up Sugarloaf. Endurance races are a microcosm of life: you're high, you're low, in the race, out of the race, crushing it, getting crushed, managing fears, rewriting stories. Fifteen minutes after I dropped Bob and his teammates, they were right with me again. We again formed a solid pack of 20 or so, and hitched up for the relatively flat terrain that would take us to Twin Lakes at mile 40, where the epic climb to the turnaround at Columbine Mine, 12,424 feet, began.

It was time to sit in and wait.

Dad emerged from the chaotic feed zone at mile 40 to hand me some bottles of Vitargo. Dad is as good as anyone at the quick athlete scan for signs of weakness. I knew he was looking at me, and I hoped he liked what he saw.

It's amazing how 10 seconds in the presence of someone who cares for you can make all the difference in the world. "It's all good mental training, Bud. Riding up this hill is going to hurt, so you might as well go hard and crush those guys, Bud. Overcome the fear, Bud. The higher you go, the stronger you get, Bud." I felt briefly like the little boy again, riding with his dad in the mountains around our home.

Channeling his energy and grit, I raced the next 10 miles in earnest, and I felt stronger and stronger as I passed a steady stream of competitors while ascending the race's biggest climb to the turnaround at Columbine Mine at 50 miles. The positive stories played out in my head; the mantras were going again.

The higher we go, the stronger we get. Come on Trav.

That worked—until we stopped going higher. For a climber like me, who doesn't possess a ton of cycling power, the flats are brutal—and that's where we were now: on the flat and rolling section between Twin Lakes and Powerline, slowly working our way back to town. What's more, I found myself battling strong winds as I worked toward the final climbs. My fear—yes, another fear!—was that Africa and Jay might be close behind in a strong pack, working with other riders to chew quickly through the time I had gained.

I hunched low to get out of the wind, cranked the heart rate up another notch, and listened to the voices: this time, those of my kids. "Go, Daddy, go." Wyatt and Lila were with me in spirit, and I knew a crucial moment like this was a good time to begin thinking about the greatest of motivators.

Powerline climbs 1,300 feet in 3.4 miles, which means the grade is around 7.3 percent, on average. Road signs here in Colorado warn drivers about climbs: "Steep hill—4% grade." So, at nearly twice that

grade, Powerline is definitely tough, especially when you're not driv-
ing a car. The top is really nefarious, because it goes on and on, passing numerous false summits en route to the high point at 11,123 feet.
Every time you think you're finally reaching the top . . . no! It just
keeps going, winding what seems like forever upward.

My task now was to ride the hill hard enough to extend or maintain my Leadman lead but easy enough to prevent bonking. When
I did this race in 2011, like many of the other top riders I stayed on
the bike all the way through the steep section. In 2013, riding was
not a possibility, because I simply didn't have the riding legs after
all of the running that summer; as at the 50 bike a month earlier, I
felt better on my feet than on the bike. So once again, I hopped off
and pushed, passing a few guys who were riding and a few more
who were also pushing. My fuel plan was working, and I could tell I
was holding strong while many competitors were falling apart. I also
tweaked my mantra:

The longer we go, the stronger we get. Come on, Trav.

Now it was my voice again, my confidence speaking, banishing
those fears, which I seemed to have left in the mountain mud miles
ago. Coming up Sixth Street into town and the finish line, I kept the
gas on. Two thousand racers in town meant even more family and
friends lining the street. Leadman race numbers are marked with a big
black "L," and people went nuts when they saw me coming. The 7:32
time kept me at the top of the Leadman leader board, although Bob
was not too far behind, at 7:56. Three down, two events to go.

LEADMAN: EVENT 4
10K RUN

No one's legs feel great the day after racing 100 miles on a mountain
bike, and despite my conservative tactics, I woke up stiff and sore like
everyone else. I fueled up with the usual combo of oatmeal, Greek
yogurt, water, Vitargo, and coffee, and soon it was time to cruise the

6.2-mile course that would become the first and last 5Ks of the following week's 100-miler. I'm not sure why they decided to stick a 10K in the middle of these 100-milers, but my coach, Josiah Middaugh, and I had decided early in the summer that racing hard in the 10K run would be unwise. Hammering it could possibly degrade the already-tired legs enough for me to lose five or ten hours next week in the real race.

Nonetheless, watching Africa, Jay, Peinado, and a few of the other Leadman competitors float away from me during the 10K prompted the voice of fear to start talking once again:

Maybe they really are that much stronger than me. Maybe they'll be able to really smoke me next week.

That voice lingered. Going into the final event, I was still about 1 hour and 15 minutes ahead of Bob, who was in second place. That sounds like a decent lead, but huge chunks of time can be lost quickly in ultrarunning if someone gets hurt or just runs out of gas. I knew Bob, Luke, and some of the other Leadman competitors were tough and experienced runners, and the series win was by no means in the bag. Particularly unsettling was that Bob had done well in many 100-mile runs—and this was my first one.

LEADMAN: FINAL EVENT
LEADVILLE 100 RUN

A week later, I lined up with around 1,000 other runners at 4:00 a.m. on the familiar corner of Sixth and Harrison in Leadville. The race had grown, and corporate sponsorships had hyped up the atmosphere since my dad had run it in the 1980s and 1990s. BOOM. I was shaken out of my reminiscence by Ken Chlouber's starting shotgun blast. Some things never change.

One hundred miles. That's a long way to run. Heck, it's a long way to drive. It would be like running from Philadelphia to New York City and then doing 3 miles around Central Park for good measure. If

Whether it's the sunrise start of the Leadville 100 bike or the still-nighttime gun blast of the 100 run a week later, seen here, the atmosphere at Leadville is always electric. I was stoked to line up for my first 100-mile run as the last event of the Leadville Race Series in 2013. CREDIT: JAN DEPUY

you're going to run such a distance, you sure as hell better break it into manageable chunks. Particularly since this was my first 100-mile run, my general plan was to start conservatively, not get caught up in the racing early on, and tackle the course step by step, focusing on getting to the next aid station rather than worrying about the entire course. At each aid station, I would grab a fuel bottle, a water bottle, some food, and dry clothing (if needed) from my crew. I wouldn't stop to talk, but seeing my friends and family would give me a nice boost.

Things went smoothly enough for me over the first 60 miles at Leadville. I chatted with other runners in the dark until the first aid station at 13 miles, and then climbed and descended conservatively over the Powerline climb I had done in the bike race, reaching the Outward Bound aid station (so-called because it's located on the

Aid station efficiency and effectiveness are key to a good performance at supported ultra runs like Leadville. We planned ahead carefully, and my family knew just what I would be looking for at each crew point. Credit: Jan DePuy

grounds of Leadville's Outward Bound school) after around a marathon. In the field of about 1,000, I had been somewhere in the 30s, and I moved up a bit en route to Twin Lakes at 40 miles. As I climbed from Twin Lakes at 9,210 feet to Hope Pass at 12,540 feet, I passed more competitors.

The higher we go, the stronger we get.

As we dropped down the other side of Hope, though, the temperature rose significantly. You don't expect heat to be the great challenge at a race high in the mountains, so this was a surprise. And I was running out of water. Refilling at Winfield, mile 50, I was enthused to see my family . . . though I didn't consider following Dad's lead with a relaxed picnic. I headed right back out on the trail, and then ran out of water yet again. Over the next few miles, I slowed down. Bob and Luke both caught me as I ran down from Hope Pass.

Sixty miles into the run, the race for Leadman was on! Our crews plus the crowd of some 100 people erupted as the three of us came in together to the Twin Lakes aid station. Ultra finishes are often separated by hours, so seeing the three top Leadman athletes running together after 60 miles made for exciting action.

The Leadman series title was still anyone's game.

Winning would require a solid finish, and I could tell Bob and Luke were both moving well, effortlessly ticking off 7:30 miles as we covered the flats between the bottom of Hope and Twin Lakes. I rushed through the aid station, knowing every moment mattered, and soon found myself back on the trail, first climbing steeply for a few miles and then heading for around 10 miles of relatively flat terrain that would bring me back to the Outward Bound aid station; I'd have a mountainous marathon to get to the finish line from there.

Then I ran into problems. I was pushing hard in order to gap Bob and Luke as I climbed ahead of them on the steep Colorado Trail heading north to the base of Mt. Elbert, Colorado's highest peak at 14,439 feet.

I had become mildly dehydrated. It was still hot out, and the sun beat down without reprieve. I had been running for more than 13 hours, and I still had more than 50 kilometers to go: 31 miles—an entire ultra! This was farther than I'd ever run before, and I was feeling nauseous. Soon, I was barely running. And then Bob passed me; he looked great, moving his feet quickly and chatting happily with his pacer.

"Hey Trav, roll with me here!" Bob is a nice guy, and I knew he was genuine in the invitation to run alongside him and work together.

"Nice work, Bob!" I tried to sound confident and pick up my stride. "See you up there in a minute."

But I knew I wouldn't. Bob cruised away from me, and I was left shuffling and suffering on the trail. I was bonking and the competition was running away. The way things looked, Bob would easily overcome his series time deficit between here and the finish line. I'd be the also-ran in the competition I'd dreamed about winning.

Then, a voice in my head. And it wasn't the Ultra Mindset speaking:

You've run 70 miles, farther than you ever have in one push in your life; there's no way you're going to start running any faster than you are right now.

The writing was on the wall: the next aid station would be as good of a place as any to quit. I plodded along, thinking about how I could explain myself to Dad when he pulled up in his truck a few miles ahead:

My legs are trashed and I'm dehydrated. Every step is painful. I can't get any food down. Bob passed me and he's looking really strong . . . so much for the Leadman title, let alone a record time. I really wanted to be a Leadman, but this is too much suffering.

I realized I was rationalizing—defined by Webster's as "devising plausible explanations for (one's acts, beliefs, etc.), usually in self-deception." Yes, I was devising and deceiving myself. And that's especially easy to do when things get tough. I was, indeed, tired, a little dehydrated, and possibly out of contention for the Leadman win, but—once I'd gulped down some fluids—none of those would be legitimate reasons to quit.

There was no need to quit, and so I wouldn't.

Don't quit.

It became my mantra, and I kept running.

Don't quit.

I kept running, and I felt a bit better.

Don't quit.

I kept running, the sun set, and I cooled down.

Don't quit.

I kept running, and my positive stories returned. The wild track was loud and clear. Suffering into the night, I focused on *why* instead of *what*. I remembered the 4:30 a.m. Rule and my commitment to myself, and I thought of my ego and my carrots and all of the guys I wanted to be like and how they had all endured stuff just like this. I remembered that, at the heart of the matter, this really was some excellent mental training.

As the finish line approached ever so slowly during the cold night hours, I thought about my family and friends waiting up ahead. I ran a little bit faster when recalling that a Leadman win would not only be a victory for me but for Amy, her mother Sandy, and my mom, who had all juggled their schedules without complaint over the past three years to make sure I had time to train and our kids were loved and cared for. I thought about what I would tell my own kids when they were old enough to understand. Most of all, I thought about Dad shuffling up the never-ending boulevard to the finish line that

Although only one person officially finishes, endeavors like Leadman are always a group effort. It was great to celebrate with family and friends in the middle of that cold mountain night (*left to right*: pacer Jason Poole, Katelyn Macy, pacer Rob Harsh, pacer Scott Swaney, Amy Macy [holding Lila], me, Dona Macy, Dad, Mom, Uncle Tim DePuy [also a Leadville 100 Run finisher], and Aunt Michelle Macy). CREDIT: JAN DEPUY

first time years ago, in last place with legs trashed but spirit unfazed. I took those same steps that night with tears in my eyes and happiness in my heart.

In short, I mobilized the entire Ultra Mindset to help me get through the last few miles of the biggest race of my life. It was an unstoppable force.

I had pushed hard enough to finish the run in fifteenth place overall with a time of 20 hours, 15 minutes. When all was said and done, over the course of the Leadville Race Series I had run and biked 282.4 miles and climbed 44,951 feet in 36 hours and 20 minutes. I had won the series and set a new record.

I hadn't quit. I was the winner. I was a Leadman.

Ultra Mindset 8: Never Quit . . . Except When You Should Quit

HERE'S WHAT IT COMES DOWN TO: IF YOU'RE DOING SOMETHING you really care about, something you know aligns with your true self and highest purposes in life, never quit because you fear what will happen if you continue. Fear will be there, and that's just part of the deal—keep going anyway. Failure is the worst possible outcome, and that's not all too bad given that everyone who puts himself out there is bound to fail, often regularly, on the path to success. Finishing Leadman aligned with who I want to be and how I want to spend my life, so quitting was not an option.

On the other hand, if you are doing something you come to know as incongruent with your true self and highest purposes, odds are that you are continuing to do it because fear tells you *not* to quit. You're afraid of what will happen if you quit. Or because other people tell you to keep going. Or because making money has somehow become more important than being happy. Or because you made a decision long ago to pursue a certain path and can't come to grips with changing your mind. If you are doing something with your life that you don't want to do, then QUIT. True courage is overcoming fear and spending your life in what you believe to be a purposeful manner. A year and a half later, I joke with friends that I'm "proud to be a drop-out" after quitting the principal licensure program. The truth is much more serious: I'm *damn* glad I quit something I was doing out of fear that would have set me up for a life I did not want.

People often quit endeavors in which they really should persevere because they're afraid of the enormity of what lies ahead. If you want to achieve the goal, and you are ready to commit, break the process into manageable steps.

In my work with high school students, one of my most important roles is to help them gain and maintain motivation and ensure that they enter the real world with the work habits and mindset necessary for success in academics, work, and life in general. With this in mind, I work often with them on practicing the strategy of breaking large challenges into manageable chunks. Need to write an essay? Create an outline, draft, edit, revise, and finalize. Want to earn a high score on the Advanced Placement Calculus test? You're not going to learn it all in one night, so study chapter by chapter, gaining mastery over each concept as you go. Feeling overwhelmed by the pile of work in front of you during finals week? Make a checklist (including when and where you will accomplish each item), and then simply go down the list without even thinking about the entire body of work.

Fear is one of the most powerful forces that keeps people from taking on and/or overcoming significant challenges. When something seems too hard, we simply avoid it by not even starting in the first place. Thankfully, one of the most effective ways to keep fear at bay is using the exact strategy that's so important to high school students: break your large and challenging task into manageable chunks, just as I did in the Leadman ultra-endurance series.

This strategy is imminently applicable in almost every aspect of life. Sometimes, we quit something big, such as a certain career track, in order to drastically impact our life direction. Other times, continuing forward in a meaningful direction requires quitting pursuits, activities, and actions that hinder progress with regard to the greater goal. In his excellent 2001 business text, *Good to Great: Why Some Companies Make the Leap . . . and Others Don't,* Jim Collins and his team introduced the Stop Doing List, which asks us to identify things we need to, well . . . stop doing in order to become great. If I'm running a small business, for example, I might stop doing my own taxes and accounting and instead pay a professional to do them, because I can make more money in the extra time I spend running the business.

I'm always looking for compelling books related to education and motivation, and in addition to Collins's, I have recently appreciated some of the points William Deresiewicz made in 2014 in *Excellent Sheep: The Miseducation of the American Elite and the Way to a Meaningful Life.* While the book has sparked controversy in many circles for his critique of the elite university system in America, Deresiewicz's advice to young people resonates with what we've been saying here and what I tell my students. To get to a higher purpose and deeper life and intentional existence, Deresiewicz suggests a few options most people usually run away from: moving *toward fear, quitting* the natural course, and *failing* regularly.

If fear lies ahead, then you must be pushing your limits and growing. You moved toward fear every single day when you were a little kid doing things for the first time, and consequently you grew and matured. Now, keep growing and maturing! What seems to be the natural course or direction for you may have been determined by your parents or by what you wanted to do when you were in ninth grade or by what you wanted to do ten years ago. It's time to give it some thought: if your boat is headed where you want to go, paddle hard; if not, then by all means change direction! And if you never fail, then odds are that you are not shooting high enough, because you're stuck in a comfort zone you've already mastered. Some of the people I've mentioned in this book—Mike Kloser, Josiah Middaugh, Danelle Ballengee, Dave Mackey, Emma Roca, me—have won a lot of races over many years. All of us, though, have lost far more races than we've won. If you want to go big, failing repeatedly is part of the deal.

Said otherwise, don't quit because you're afraid of something you really want to do. Do quit if you're on a less-than-ideal course and you're afraid of what will happen if you change directions.

Mindset 8 REFLECTION

Sometimes we quit without really thinking about what we're doing, and other times we keep slogging forward without even analyzing whether the course is a good one. One effective way to carefully consider whether you should start something new, continue what you're doing, or quit all together is to take a very close look at your fears, which—consciously or not—play a big role in the decisions we make. Here's a three-step guide for assessing (and maybe banishing) your fears.

To start, write down something you want to do or are thinking about doing; this is the change you're contemplating, the decision you are mulling over. Remember, this could be about starting something (running your first 10K, asking someone on a date), about continuing something (completing the law school program you've already started, finishing an ultra when you're really suffering), or about quitting something (dropping your full-time gig to start a new business, relocating from a place you know to somewhere new).

I want to: _____.

_____

_____

1) Now list the fears that are keeping you from doing it.

(If you need help articulating these, see the list of common fears below the exercise.)

"I am afraid of doing this because . . . "

. . . _____

_____.

. . . _____

_____.

. . . _____

_____.

. . . _____

_____.

. . . _____

_____.

. . . _____

_____.

2) For each of the fears you have listed, create a new story. It could be a rational response to that specific fear, a way to neutralize or overcome it, or just a positive mantra, like the "Don't quit, keep it consistent" mantra that I used in the final stage of Leadman.

New stories responding to each of your fears:

_____

_____ .

_____

_____ .

_____

_____ .

_____

_____ .

_____

_____ .

_____

_____ .

3) So, where do you go from here? How do you know if your fears are enough to hold you back from the endeavor that's challenging you?

Take a look at your new stories and what you have learned, and check the box that applies.

____ A. Pursuing this endeavor aligns with my true self and higher purposes in life.

___ B. Pursuing this endeavor does not align with my true self and higher purposes in life.

If you chose A, then keep going. If you chose B, then you might want to consider quitting.

Some common fears:

I'm afraid my performance won't live up to all the hard work I put in.

I'm afraid the process or experience I'm about to undergo is too intense, too new, too uncomfortable, or something similar.

I'm afraid the suffering is too much right now.

I'm afraid I'll suffer too much in the future if I do this.

I'm afraid that if I fail I will have trouble dealing with it.

I'm afraid that if I fail someone else will have trouble dealing with it.

I'm afraid that if I fail I'll know I'm not good enough.

I'm afraid this endeavor does not align with my greater goals in life.

I'm afraid that I'm not capable of doing it or qualified to do it.

I'm afraid that continuing is not best for my family.

I'm afraid of quitting because I have an "I don't quit policy."

I followed these three steps to complete the biggest race of my career. I not only wanted to complete the Leadville Race Series, I wanted to win it and set a new record for the series.

What was holding me back for a while during this process? Fear. Fear is a powerful force, perhaps the single most compelling factor that prevents people from meeting their potential and living life to its fullest—on their own terms. Fear acts by preventing people from doing what they want to do and, just as significantly, compelling them to keep doing what they *don't* want to do.

Fear can also creep up on you. I was confident when I was setting my goals, but as the races got closer that summer, I found myself beset by fears—a wide range of them, which I listed at the time, just as I've recommended you do:

> I was afraid the bike training would hurt my running.
> I was afraid the run training would hurt my biking.
> I was afraid the run and bike training would hurt my family.
> I was afraid I might get hurt.
> I was afraid I might train too much.
> I was afraid I might not train enough.
> I was afraid all of the little aches and pains I always have were turning into real injuries.
> I was afraid sleep deprivation from raising an infant and camping before races with two kids would slow me down.
> I was afraid other competitors would outperform me.
> I was afraid I might not win.
> I was afraid, in many ways, of the entire Leadman concept.

Some list, huh? Enough maybe to have kept me from even attempting Leadman in the first place. I needed positive stories, and I needed them fast. Luckily, I had them ready. My inner voice speaks to me in second person, and this is what I heard:

> You're doing something important.
> You may not have run 100 miles before, but you have the experience needed.
> You are training wisely.
> You have trained enough.
> You are setting a good example for your kids.
> You have a winning mindset.
> You know how to fuel your body and take care of yourself.

You are ready for the altitude.

You'll have fun. Or something like it.

You'll be proud of yourself.

Your dad will be proud.

You can win; you will win.

This positive self-talk gave me confidence that the decision to take on the Leadman challenge at this point in my life was a sound one. But clearly, finishing Leadman would be an extended exercise in fear management. My positive stories and good training could get me to the start line. But winning it, I knew from the moment I signed up, would be a true test of my Ultra Mindset from start to finish; the only route to success was to prevent fear from ruling my thoughts and dictating my actions.

Rock star David Bowie once sang about being "ready to shape the scheme of things." What a great line! I like to think I shaped the circumstances of my life to allow me to compete in and win the greatest athletic challenge of my life. Are you ready to shape the scheme of things in your life, your career, your running, or your other endeavors? You start by assessing the fears, as I did, and then by addressing them with a new outlook, a new resolve, and a new perspective.

Mindset 8 ACTIVITY: Just for Fun Run

Whether you're running, biking, or participating in another type of exercise, you're not likely to stick with it for long if you're not having fun . . . even just a little! Here are some ways to make endurance more enjoyable.

Mental growth: One key element to maintaining enthusiasm for something you are dedicated to and do not want to quit is finding times to have fun doing it. Sometimes it's important to be intentional about having fun. I believe in a "fun transference" between various areas of life; in other words, going for a fun run, hike, bike ride (or even dinner out with friends, for that matter) can reenergize you for, say, your professional work.

Physical growth: If you're like me, you probably find yourself in an exercise rut at times, completing your training but doing almost the same runs or rides day after day. Intentionally choosing a route or experience based purely on fun will not only refresh your mind but probably also provide a varied physiological stimulus (in other words, something new for your body).

When: A good "rule of fun" is to train just for fun at least once every week or two. I particularly like to incorporate training for fun during the weeks after a big race, when less structure in training facilitates mental and physical recovery.

How: These strategies help me boost the fun factor in training:

Go somewhere new. Variety is the spice of life, and it's even tastier if you go somewhere beautiful. Is there a new trail, a new bike path, even a neighborhood with quiet, wide streets that you've never explored? Instead of going to the "regular spot" to start, go to the irregular, the new, the different. You might find that a whole new running route opens up for you.

Don't wear a watch. Complete a given route for the sake of joy and a sense of accomplishment, without worrying about how long it takes or how far you go.

Take your dog with you . . . or borrow someone else's. I don't know about you, but seeing how excited my dogs are to go for a run always makes me glad to be getting out the door.

Bring back a classic. If you've been at the training game for a while, try bringing out an old race t-shirt, your favorite bike shorts from when you first started, those lime green 1980s running tights you forgot about, some shoes you haven't worn recently, or even a humorous outfit of some sort (especially if you're meeting friends).

Find a new running (biking, hiking, etc.) buddy (or two). Despite the myth of the Loneliness of the Long Distance Runner, we runners tend to be quite sociable. Many of us have friends we like to train and converse with. Maybe this week, you ask someone *new*—a runner you've met at races, a friend of a friend's, a colleague, if they'd like to join you. Just enjoy running together while enjoying the pleasure of making a new friend. That's fun!

Find a cause (fundraiser, platform, event, etc.) that you care about and run or bike in honor of that cause. Fundraising and cause-related races and training programs abound these days; go out and find one to make a difference while boosting your own motivation.

Extra: To increase fun and newness, make a point of doing things differently than you usually do. If you usually train with a watch, train without during your fun session. If you always listen to music, try leaving it at home in favor of paying attention to your thoughts and surroundings. If you typically run or ride a loop in one direction, go the other way. If you usually train on the hills, try the flats, or vice versa. If you usually go with a group, get out there alone, and vice versa. The point is to mix it up and enjoy some originality!

Mindset 8 LEARN

Robyn Benincasa

RACING LIFE

Robyn is one of America's original adventure-racing legends, having graced the podiums of the Eco-Challenge and Raid Gauloises in the 1990s and 2000s. Robyn and I raced together toward the end of her career with Team Merrell, finishing second at Primal Quest Montana in 2008. In addition to being a world champion adventure racer, Robyn is also a Guinness World Record kayaker and stand-up paddler and a multiple Ironwoman (see www.worldclassteams.com).

REAL LIFE

Robyn is always on the go outside of racing as well. When she's not leading an all-female firefighting unit in California, she's working as a successful entrepreneur, *New York Times* best-selling author (*How Winning Works*, 2012), and founder and "minister of dreams" for the Project Athena Foundation, a nonprofit that supports women who have endured life-altering medical setbacks as they pursue and achieve athletic goals and newfound empowerment.

ROBYN'S THOUGHTS ON OVERCOMING FEAR TO AVOID QUITTING SOMETHING YOU CARE ABOUT

How many times in our lives have we put something off because we're not ready, we need more time, we don't feel comfortable, and so on? I've completed 10 Ironman Triathlons and more than 40 ten-day, nonstop adventure races through the most remote places on earth. Here's a secret: I didn't feel "ready" for any of them, and I was always afraid of something.

There was always more I could have done to train, something I needed more time to prepare, or I wished I could delay the start until a day when I felt stronger. Truth be told, I would most likely never have approached a start line or undertaken those "risks" to journey into the unknown—physically, emotionally, and interpersonally—if there hadn't been a specific date on the calendar and someone with a megaphone saying "go!" But I am ever so glad I did.

So how do we stop "wishing" we had more guts and inspire ourselves to overcome the fear and ditch the vanilla life for a big, satisfying scoop of rocky road less traveled?

(continues)

Step into Character

Nobody knows what's going on inside your head but you. Remember that to the outside world you appear 100 percent to be the businessperson, triathlete, writer, or other achiever you always wanted to be (enter your dream here). View yourself the way you want people to see you: confident, smart, talented. Then, BE that person. For example, I'm the biggest introvert on earth, and I'm a speaker for a living. How? Right before I go on stage, I think about the person everyone in the audience is expecting to meet (vs. little scared me!), and the moment they invite me onto the stage, I become her.

Do It Anyway

How you feel is far less important than what you DO. Feeling scared, nervous, and uncomfortable when you're rappelling off that symbolic cliff is just a GIVEN. It's the price of admission for an exceptional life! The only difference between you and the person who is living his or her dream is that that person felt the fear and did it anyway. Fear will always be there when we face risks. In fact, I've come to embrace fear as the vigilant guardian and trusted friend that gives me a "heads-up" to be at my best.

—Robyn

Epilogue

The Colorado Rockies

OCTOBER 2014

I'm cruising along a washboard dirt road through the lodgepole pines here in Evergreen, the snow-covered peaks of the Rockies in early autumn framed in the background. Next to me is three-year-old Wyatt on his mountain bike, hammering the hills as I do my best Phil Liggett impression. Yes, I'm learning, we *do* become our parents. Reflecting back on how a quarter century earlier, it would have been me on training wheels, and Dad beside me, on one of our mental training missions, I think about the Ultra Mindset and what it means to Wyatt, my family—and you.

My kids will be old enough to make decisions for themselves before I know it, and I hope they'll consider some of the advice from Dad and Grandpa Macy, in addition to adding their personal flair to any given situation. Just as my interest in endurance racing evolved naturally, I'm certainly not going to push my kids into it. But I do want them to be happy and to make the most of life however they see fit. And I know that the Ultra Mindset will help them do that, whether or not they become ultra-endurance athletes.

That's true for you as well. Although it will surely increase your likelihood of achieving your goals, the Ultra Mindset doesn't guarantee success. That's not what it's all about anyway; anyone who goes big—and I hope you will use this book to do just that in your own way, and shoot for the most challenging goals—knows that failing is part of the deal sometimes.

Indeed, the Ultra Mindset tells us as much about dealing with setbacks as it does about how to win.

Maybe you love fly fishing or yoga or hiking. Maybe you feel alive when you're teaching kids or being with family or traveling solo. Maybe your soul soars when you're lawyering or campaigning or working on Wall Street. Whatever it is, whatever gives you purpose in life, that's where you want to spend your time—and that's where you want to apply the Ultra Mindset.

So, take what you've learned and jump into action, going big (and doing so relentlessly) with whatever brings love and fulfillment into your life. I'll be up here in the mountains, rooting for you, as I continue on the racing adventures that have defined my life and made me a better person.

That's my Ultra Mindset story. Now what's yours?

Travis Macy
with John Hanc

John (left) and I (right) thoroughly enjoyed writing this book. We appreciate you joining our journey, and we wish you the best with the Ultra Mindset! CREDIT: ALEXANDRE GARIN

The Finish Line!

Thanks for going the distance with *The Ultra Mindset*. If you made it this far, you might also be interested in some of the resources available at www.travismacy.com:

- ‣ Trav's Email Newsletter (it's free), where I share monthly about mindset, racing, training, and life
- ‣ Motivational speaking examples and booking information
- ‣ Instructional videos on a wide range of training and racing topics
- ‣ Endurance coaching details and pricing
- ‣ Independent college counseling information

I really do love hearing from readers, so please get in touch with me through www.travismacy.com or @travismacy.

Acknowledgments

Writing a book is like doing an ultra run, an adventure race, or a 24-hour mountain-bike race. The highs and lows are intense, and you only make it through by believing in yourself, figuring out unforeseen challenges when they arrive, and holding true to your initial commitment no matter what.

Endurance racing, even in solo events, is always a group effort. You must ask for help in learning how to train, staying motivated, and setting up your life and schedule to make time for hours each day out in the hills. Likewise, no one writes a book alone. I started this book by making a commitment to myself late one night while camping solo high in the Rocky Mountains in July 2013. And then I started asking for help.

Marshall and Heather Ulrich got me going by sharing experiences related to writing Marshall's excellent book, *Running on Empty*. My CU-Boulder running teammate, Matt McCue, who wrote *An Honorable Run*, was also very helpful in providing initial guidance. When I had no connections in the writing industry, author Steve Friedman took my call, provided valuable advice, and connected me to a great agent, Daniel Greenberg, with the Levine

Greenberg Rostan Literary Agency. I appreciate Da Capo Press taking me on, and Dan Ambrosio and his team were constantly supportive and more than understanding with my naïve questions about the business of writing a book. Dean Karnazes shared valuable time and effort in providing an excellent and much-appreciated Foreword.

I would like to thank John Hanc, who started as my co-writer and became my friend and teacher. His perspective, skill, work ethic, and patience have been invaluable.

My adventure racing teammates and training partners past and present taught me more about life than any book or class could offer; this book could not exist without each and every one of them. Likewise, various sponsors over the years (most recently, Vitargo and Hoka One One) have allowed me to race around the world. Every company has people behind it—you know who you are, and I appreciate your support. As you've seen in the book, many athletes and photographers were generous with their wisdom, time, and energy in making this book come to life.

Mom, Sandy, and Amy, thank you for supporting my chaotic schedule and multifaceted professional life by providing love and care for our kids at random times so I can go running and biking. Most of this book was written (or at least thought about) out on the trails, and it could not have happened without you.

Mom and Dad, you live on every page. Amy, Wyatt, and Lila, you are my reason for this and all else. Ryan Haebe, our runs together around our small town in the mountains during your recovery from traumatic brain injury, when I was supposedly helping you, meant more to me than you will ever know. Thank you for reminding me to spend my life doing things I care about and to help people by sharing what I have learned through racing.

Appendix:
The Ultra Mindset at a Glance

MINDSET 1: IT'S ALL GOOD MENTAL TRAINING

Viewing your challenges as positive, essential elements of building a winning mindset makes all the difference in the world. When the going gets tough, tell yourself, "This is good mental training." Which it is: Remember that self-control can be trained, just like any other muscle.

MINDSET 2: BE A WANNABE

Get close to the people you want to be like—make the most of *goal contagion*. By identifying people you would like to emulate in one or more ways, you can find examples of people who are reaching goals similar to your own. Utilize the synergy and push each other.

MINDSET 3: FIND YOUR CARROT

Utilize extrinsic motivators—such as money, utilitarian purpose, glory, and admiration—especially when the self-control muscle tires. Intrinsic motivation—doing something because you enjoy it in the moment—is also important, and you better have it if you want to do anything big. For the greatest challenges, though, it can be good to keep extrinsic carrots in mind.

MINDSET 4: HAVE AN EGO AND USE IT—UNTIL IT'S TIME TO PUT YOUR EGO ASIDE

Accomplishing big goals requires perseverance, and that requires a high view of self. The Ultra Mindset often requires taking on great challenges that we may have no business tackling. In such cases, belief in what you are capable of doing can help you succeed in doing it. But when you need assistance, don't let that ego stand in your way: ask for help!

MINDSET 5: THINK ABOUT YOUR THINKING: *WHAT* AND *WHY*

Program yourself to think about the right things at the right time. If something is particularly detail-oriented (such as editing a professional document, creating a business plan, or climbing a precipitous mountain), think about *what* you are doing to increase effectiveness and avoid errors. When things get drawn-out and grueling on a Friday afternoon at work or at mile 24 of your marathon, tune out the monotonous, painful *what* with a focus on *why* you are doing it.

MINDSET 6: THE 4:30 A.M. RULE: WHEN YOU HAVE NO CHOICE, ANYTHING IS POSSIBLE

When the alarm goes off at 4:30 a.m., literally or figuratively, get up and take action. You committed ahead of time, and whether or not you feel like doing it (whatever "it" may be) in the moment doesn't really matter if you're working toward something aligned with your higher purposes in life. A 4:30 a.m. moment can happen at any time, and the more you follow through on previous commitments when push comes to shove, the easier it becomes to do so regularly.

MINDSET 7: BAD STORIES, GOOD STORIES: THE ONES YOU TELL YOURSELF MAKE ALL THE DIFFERENCE

The ongoing dialogue that plays out in our heads can be channeled in the right direction. Negative stories must be rewritten and fought with better ones. These can be nothing more than positive mantras—"I am getting stronger with each step"—that can be cued up in your mind to replace the negative ones—"I can't take another step." A key first step is to recognize your negative stories for what they are—just stories and nothing more.

MINDSET 8: NEVER QUIT . . . EXCEPT WHEN YOU SHOULD QUIT

If you're doing something you really care about, something that you know aligns with your true self and highest purposes in life, don't quit just because you fear what will happen if you continue. Fear will be there, and that's just part of the deal—keep going anyway. On the other hand, if you are doing something with your life that does not align with who you want to be and how you want to live, then maybe you should quit. True courage is overcoming fear to spend your life in what you believe to be a purposeful manner.

About the Authors

Finisher of more than 100 ultradistance competitions in 16 countries, **Travis Macy** is a professional endurance athlete who produces world-class results due primarily to an exceptional mindset. His racing exploits have been covered by the *New York Times*, *Runner's World*, *Adventure Sports*, *Competitor*, *UltraRunning*, *Trail Runner*, and *Breathe*, among others. A sought-after motivational speaker, Macy also coaches endurance athletes, writes about racing and travel, and provides independent college counseling, including writing instruction and test prep, to high school students. He lives in Evergreen, Colorado, with his wife and two young children.

John Hanc is a longtime contributing writer and columnist for *Newsday* and a contributing editor to *Runner's World* magazine. He is the author of 12 previous books, including the award-winning memoir *The Coolest Race on Earth* about his experience running the Antarctica Marathon. Hanc, who also teaches journalism at the New York Institute of Technology in Old Westbury, New York, has run 28 career marathons and resides in Farmingdale, New York, with his wife and son.

Index